# A Better
# Home Life

**A code of good
practice for
residential and
nursing home care**

**Report of an Advisory
Group convened by the
Centre for Policy on
Ageing and chaired by
Kina, Lady Avebury**

First published in 1996 by the
Centre for Policy on Ageing
25-31 Ironmonger Row
London EC1V 3QP

©1996 Centre for Policy on Ageing

British Library Cataloguing-in-
Publication Data.
A catalogue record for this book is
available from the British Library.

ISBN 0 904139 91 3

Designed and typeset by The Perfect
Design Company.
Printed by TWP Services Ltd, London.

# Contents

# Advisory Group members

Kina, Lady Avebury, *Chairwoman*

Professor Tom Arie, *Psychiatrist, lately Professor of Health Care of the Elderly, University of Nottingham*

David Brown, *Chief Executive, Quantum Care Limited* and *Chairman, The Care Forum*

Dr Michael Denham, *Consultant Physician in Geriatric Medicine, Harrow and Hillingdon Healthcare NHS Trust*

Pauline Ford, *Advisor in Nursing and Older People, Royal College of Nursing*

Brian Jones, *Association of Metropolitan Authorities*

Leonie Kellaher, *Director, Centre for Environmental and Social Studies in Ageing, University of North London*

Professor Mary Marshall, *Director, Dementia Services Development Centre, University of Stirling*

Foster Murphy, *Chief Executive, The Abbeyfield Society*

Anne Parker, *Simon Research Fellow, Department of Social Policy and Social Work, University of Manchester*

Pat Ramdhanie, *Chair, Society of Nurse Inspection and Registration Officers*

Bryan Rowe, *Manager, Assynt Centre, Lochinver, Department of Social Work, Highland Regional Council*

Sheila Scott, *Chief Executive, National Care Homes Association*

Martin Shreeve, *Director of Social Services, Wolverhampton Metropolitan Borough Council*

Jef Smith, *General Manager, Counsel and Care*

Jenny Stiles, *Director, The Relatives Association*

Derek Whittaker, *Chairman, Registered Nursing Home Association*

David Wigley, *Chief Executive, Methodist Homes for the Aged*

Heather Wing, *Chair, National Association of Inspection and Registration Officers* and *Association of County Councils*

## Observer

Chris Vellenoweth, *Manager, Special Projects, National Association of Health Authorities and Trusts*

## In attendance

Gillian Dalley, *Director, Centre for Policy on Ageing*

Gillian Crosby, *Deputy Director, Centre for Policy on Ageing*

Richard Hollingbery, *Visiting Policy Associate, Centre for Policy on Ageing*

# Introduction

*by Kina, Lady Avebury*

It is a privilege to have been invited by the Centre for Policy on Ageing (CPA) to renew my involvement with *Home Life* and to have acted as Chairwoman on the Advisory Group set up to support CPA in the work of producing an updated version of the code of practice on residential care and extending it to cover continuing care generally.

Twelve years have passed since the first *Home Life* was published in 1984 as the officially commissioned guidance to accompany the Registered Homes Act which came into force the following year. There have been several reprints of the original document with over 100,000 copies having been sold and it remains one of the most widely used and authoritative reference points for professional staff concerned with the well-being of vulnerable people in residential settings.

The first version of *Home Life* was directed towards two main areas of readership: firstly, to the owners and managers of residential care homes and secondly, to the newly appointed registration and inspection staff in local authority social services departments in England and Wales. The first Working Party set up by the Centre for Policy on Ageing in 1982 included two official representatives of the Department of Health and the Welsh Office social services inspectorate, and the code of practice was fully endorsed and welcomed by the then Secretaries of State. This public recognition of *Home Life* as the main source of guidance on best practice in residential care was greatly valued by the authors and it did much to ensure its widespread adoption as a credible and useful work during the years following its publication.

At the time the first *Home Life* was commissioned, there had been a rapid increase in the number of homes, both large and small, up and down the country. There had also been a number of highly publicised scandals in both the statutory and independent sectors where old or vulnerable people had suffered neglect, cruelty or exploitation. Public concern arising out of such dramatic instances led to an awareness of the need for greater accountability, better training, better understanding of different needs, more sensitive and skilled responses to these needs and, most of all, care based upon respect for residents and an acknowledgement of their rights.

Nothing in the field of social care stands still, however, and twelve years on there is a general consensus amongst those who welcomed the original *Home Life* that an updated code of practice is needed. *A Better Home Life* is CPA's response.

The major pressures to look again at *Home Life* have been external ones. The Registered Homes Act 1984 has been amended to cover homes for fewer than four people. The NHS and Community Care Act 1990 has had enormous implications for the way social services departments carry out their duty to ensure that appropriate financial support and care is provided to vulnerable people. This Act reflects, in part at least, the wide-ranging and radical analysis of the Wagner committee's report and the late Sir Roy Griffiths' green paper on care in the community. The trend in these two very significant reports was to regard residential care as just one option in a range of choices that people make in a marketplace of evenly distrib-uted commodities.

The countervailing influences are, of course, related to resources, financial and human, and to the constant processes of managing these through periods of changes in culture and organisation. The NHS reforms, mirrored in other sectors, of splitting into purchasing and providing units, have led, not always smoothly, to an acceptance of the esoteric processes of commissioning and contracting for services. As these processes become increasingly refined into higher art forms, and as ends in themselves, there is a danger that the people for whom the whole edifice exists will become less than the prime focus of concern. This new code of practice is one important attempt to ensure that the primacy of residents is enshrined in service specifications and contractual arrangements whether between a home and the resident or between the home and the statutory authorities.

The Centre for Policy on Ageing and the Advisory Group feel very firmly that much of the original code applies as strongly in 1996 as it did in 1984. The underpinning values of respect, dignity, autonomy and fulfilment, to name the key ones, are relevant and central to the givers and recipients of care. There are, however, some important differences between this new version of the code and the original. This time, we have decided to direct our work exclusively towards older people, covering the whole range of needs amongst the elderly and the very old. This is in acknowledgement of recent demographic changes in the population and growing awareness of the particular needs of people suffering from dementia, who may not always be able to express personal choices about their lives or care. To have attempted to address the specific needs of other client groups at the same time as extending the discussion on the care of elderly people would, in our view, have risked the danger of bland generalisation and superficiality.

We have also decided to broaden the range of residential settings in this code of practice. The original code covered residential care homes, including those which were dually registered to provide nursing care. This code addresses the issues as they broadly affect sheltered housing, residential care homes and nursing homes. It applies to short-term and respite care services as well as continuing care till death. We hope that readers will be able to distinguish which comments and recommendations apply to which kind of resident and which kind of need. The boundaries between social, personal and nursing care are notoriously hard to define, and maybe it is a sterile exercise to over-emphasise these boundaries except where safety and professional clinical practice demand it. More important, in our view, is the holistic approach to care of people in residential settings where all the different aspects are linked by a commitment to offer the best possible quality of life.

The Advisory Group is well aware of the difficulties homeowners and managers face when they are exhorted to maintain high standards and improve unsatisfactory ones. The arguments, for example, about residents' rights to single bedrooms is a case in point. Objections were raised in 1984 against this particular recommendation and though generally accepted today, these same objections to it can still be heard. The code of practice sets out what we believe to be 'best practice' – that is, something to work towards, drawing upon the advice and counsel of registration and inspection units, as well as upon the views and wishes of residents and their families and friends.

In the present world of charters – citizens' charters and patients' charters, advocacy schemes and recognition of rights – the code recommends the attainable, not the utopian way forward. Our hope is that it will prove just as useful well into the next century as its predecessor has been over the last twelve years.

Finally, I offer my warmest thanks and appreciation to everyone who has contributed to the final document. The Advisory Group, collectively and individually, brought a range of experience, wisdom, clear-headedness and humour and gave much time to the task of producing *A Better Home Life*. Many other individuals and organisations, including the Department of Health and the major care homes associations, responded to CPA's consultation process and their contributions have been welcomed and many of them reflected in the text. The Director of CPA, Gillian Dalley, and her colleagues have carried the main responsibility for writing and editing this major piece of work. They have helped to maintain the Centre's reputation for reports which are well written, which demonstrate integrity and are, above all, readable.

# How to use the code

## 1.1    What the code covers

The code applies to the range of continuing care provided to older people by the NHS, local authorities and the independent sector. This means in particular:

- residential care homes;
- nursing homes;

and also, where appropriate, aspects of other settings such as:

- long-stay hospital wards and units;
- sheltered housing;
- sheltered housing with extra care.

It acknowledges the breadth and variety of living and care circumstances encompassed within these settings. Therefore some of the detail of the code applies more directly to some settings than to others.

*The spirit and the principles of the code, however, are relevant across the board.*

## 1.2    How it applies

The code sets out a model of good practice and describes the principles which underlie the provision of good quality care. Readers should take note of the following points:

- in the case of homes setting up for the first time, particularly where they are being newly built, it is realistic to expect the code to apply in all respects;
- the size of a home should not mean that the principles (for example, of the importance of domestic scale) are not observed;

- where standards cannot be achieved immediately (because of financial constraints, the physical limitations of existing buildings or planning and building regulations) the code should be regarded as developmental. It sets out standards which should be aspired to and achieved over time;
- legal requirements and regulations must always be observed;
- some standards which may not be required by law or regulation should nevertheless be regarded as minimum standards. It is recommended that providers meet them in all circumstances;
- arguments that financial constraints may excuse low standards and poor quality of care are never acceptable; at the same time
- funders of services should acknowledge and accept the financial implications of raised standards and quality improvement programmes.

## 1.3 Content and context

The experience of coming into care, of living in a home, of the pattern of daily life, of receiving treatment and care and ultimately of dying is encompassed in the code. Some parts of the code may be more applicable to residential homes, for example, than to nursing homes or hospital wards. Other parts may be more applicable to sheltered housing. Users of the code will need to consider the applicability of some of its aspects to their own situation. The intention is not to have unrealistic expectations of residents' capacities and inclinations but to ensure that, in whatever setting, the interests of the older people living in care are served.

## 1.4 Who should read the code

The code will be read by all those with an interest in continuing care and older people. In particular, it will be of value to:
- older people contemplating moving into care;
- their families, friends and other supporters;
- owners of homes;
- managers of homes;
- staff working in continuing care settings;
- inspectors;

- purchasers of continuing care in the statutory services;
- architects and planners;
- members of community or local health councils and other advisory organisations;
- any person involved in setting standards and assessing quality.

The model of good practice which the code sets out provides a benchmark against which existing provision can be judged. It shows prospective residents what they might reasonably expect in a good home. It offers owners and managers of homes a model of excellence to which they should aspire and actively work towards and, in certain areas, sets out standards below which they should not fall. For staff, it provides a wealth of information about how their own practice can improve. Like its predecessor, the code will also be able to be used by inspectors as a guide during their regular inspection of homes. Above all, *A Better Home Life* can be used as a basis for quality assurance for anyone working in continuing care. It sets out principles of high quality care and shows how they can be put into practice.

## 1.5 The legal framework

The code does not go into the detail of the legislation and regulations which underpin residential and nursing home care (establishments which are required to be registered) and others (sheltered housing and hospitals). Reference to these is made in the appendices and covers:

- Registered Homes Act 1984 (and subsequent amendments);
- regulations (as applied to residential care homes and nursing homes);
- NHS and Community Care Act 1990;
- Mental Health Act 1983;
- health and safety requirements;
- the National Association of Health Authorities and Trusts (NAHAT) guidelines for nursing homes;
- other regulations and guidance relating to buildings;
- legislation and guidance for Scotland and for Northern Ireland where it differs from that for England and Wales;
- Court of Protection, Court of Session, High Court;
- employment law.

## 1.6 Glossary

Many terms and words have specific meaning within the residential and nursing home context. Some relate to the law and regulations, others may be used by professionals or health and social services agencies in ways which may not always be clear to the general public. In some instances, the code has made decisions about usage for the purposes of clarity and consistency.

The following glossary of terms sets out the most commonly used:

- *fit person* – a person deemed suitable to be registered under the Registered Homes Act 1984;
- *person in charge* – the person responsible for the day-to-day management of the care of residents;
- *manager* – the person who may be the responsible person in charge of day-to-day care in a residential care home or the person who may be concerned solely with business or financial affairs of the home;
- *resident* – a person living in a residential care home or nursing home or other continuing care setting;
- *assessment* – the process led by the social services/work department in which a person's needs for services are considered;
- *care manager* – the person organising care services for an individual whose needs have been assessed;
- *key worker* – a member of staff who is given prime responsibility for ensuring that a resident is looked after in all respects;
- *care plans* – a written statement setting out what care and support a resident needs and how it is organised;
- *registration* – the formal process of ensuring that only those who are suitable in all aspects to offer care to vulnerable people are awarded a 'licence to trade';
- *inspection* – the process of ensuring on a periodic basis that certain establishments in all sectors of care continue to meet agreed standards and appropriate legal requirements;
- *inspection and registration unit* – an independent body located within a local authority or health authority that regulates a wide range of care services, having the duty to inspect establishments and with enforcement powers;

- *dual registration* – where homes are registered both with the local authority (for residential care) and the health authority (for nursing care).

Differences in terminology between Scotland and Northern Ireland and England and Wales are pointed out in the text.

## 1.7 Status of terms

- *must* is used to apply to something laid down by law or required by medical direction;
- *should* denotes good practice which is expected in most circumstances. Exceptions need good reason;
- *may* denotes good practice which is not of highest priority and is not always applicable.

# Principles of good practice

## 2.1 Introduction

Underlying all the recommendations and requirements set out in this code is a conviction that those who live in continuing care should do so with dignity, that they should have the respect of those who support them, should live with no reduction of their rights as citizens and should be entitled to live as full and active a life as their physical and mental condition will allow.

Whatever their age, whether sound in mind and body or experiencing disability, residents have a fundamental right to self-determination and individuality. Equally, they have the right to live in a manner and in circumstances which correspond as far as possible with what is normal for those who remain in their own homes. All continuing care settings should aim to enable residents to achieve their full capacity – physical, intellectual, spiritual, emotional and social – even when they have a progressive disease such as dementia. This can best be achieved by sensitive recognition and nurturing of that potential in each individual and by an understanding that it may change over time.

Residents and their well-being should be the central focus in any care setting. It is the interests of residents, individually and collectively, that should assume priority over the home, its owners, management and staff. This should mean that residents are accorded a standard of care and attention which respects individuals' privacy and dignity, recognises their diversity and individuality, fosters their independence, offers them choice and enables them to control their own lives wherever possible.

## 2.2 The principles underlying daily life in a continuing care setting

Some basic principles underlie the rights which should be accorded to all who find themselves in the care of others.

### 2.2.1 Respect for privacy and dignity

The importance of preserving the privacy and dignity of residents should be paramount. This means that they should have their own individual private space and the opportunity to choose how they dress, what they eat, when they go to bed and get up and how they spend their day. Dependence on staff for help with personal care should not mean that their dignity is compromised or that their privacy is not respected. Residents should be treated as adults, never as children. Staff should always avoid adopting patronising attitudes and behaviour towards residents. Residents should determine how they want to be addressed by staff, other residents and visitors to the home.

### 2.2.2 Maintenance of self-esteem

The preservation of self-esteem amongst those who depend on the support of others hinges upon the status they are accorded. Staff and management should not make the mistake of seeing residents only as frail old people who simply need help. They should value the contribution which individuals with their personal qualities, talents and rich experience of life can make to the life of the home. Residents' self-esteem will be enhanced if they feel valued and in this way their morale will be maintained. Staff should treat residents courteously and respect their privacy and their right to hold and express opinions or to keep them private.

### 2.2.3 Fostering of independence

It should be assumed that residents can look after themselves and handle their own affairs until it has been shown otherwise. They may need time to do things themselves but staff and relatives should resist the temptation to 'take over' unless absolutely necessary; otherwise they make residents unnecessarily dependent.

### 2.2.4 Choice and control

Wherever possible, residents should be able to make for themselves the major decisions affecting their lives. They should also be able to choose how they spend their time from day to day. For example, this means that individuals should be free to decide how far they participate in the common life of the home and how far they maintain relationships with family, friends and the local community. This exercising of choice is a right which will often require a partnership between resident, relatives and staff in which choices can be negotiated. Some residents – particularly those who are very frail and vulnerable – will need help to express their wishes and preferences. All residents should have access to external advice, representation and advocacy. Even deeply held views and aspirations may not be expressed if staff do not encourage such links outside the home. Residents should have opportunities for emotional and sexual expression and for intimate and personal relationships within and outside the home.

## 2.2.5 Recognition of diversity and individuality

Even though residents are living in a home with other people, they remain individuals with their own likes and dislikes. Staff should be responsive to the requirements of individual residents and not merely impose regimes which are dictated by the needs and preferences of the majority of residents or implemented for the convenience of managers, staff or relatives. Ethnic, cultural, social and religious diversity should be recognised as an integral part of home life. Residents should feel that their needs will be responded to willingly by staff who understand the value of maintaining a sense of continuity and identity based on past traditions and practices. For their part, living in a community with others requires that residents should recognise and respond to the rhythms and needs of other people. It may be helpful for residents to have some knowledge of the life experiences of staff to act as a bridge between them. This emphasises personal connections outside the home and their relevance to those within.

## 2.2.6 Expression of beliefs

Opportunities should be made available for religious and political beliefs to be expressed and pursued. This may involve observing particular dietary and dress requirements and facilitating practices such as prayer and contemplation which require privacy and quiet or enabling residents to attend places of worship. It may include displaying posters at election time.

### 2.2.7 Safety

Residents should be kept safe and feel safe. Wherever possible, fears and anxieties should be acknowledged and relieved while recognising at the same time that over-protectiveness and undue concern for safety may lead to infringements of personal rights.

### 2.2.8 Responsible risk-taking

Responsible risk-taking should be regarded as normal and important in maintaining autonomy and independence. Residents should not be discouraged from undertaking certain activities solely on the grounds that there is an element of risk. The balance between risk and safety has to be carefully maintained. Anxieties raised by staff and relatives should be discussed, where possible, with the individual resident concerned and agreement reached which balances the risks against the individual's rights.

### 2.2.9 Citizens' rights

Living in care does not in any way reduce residents' normal rights to statutory health and social care services. Neither are their other rights – participation in the general civic and democratic process, access to information and so on – diminished. Residents should be enabled to vote in elections if they wish to do so, in person, by post or by proxy, with full confidentiality assured.

Homes which cater for a specific group of people should ensure that admission and administrative procedures are not in conflict with any law such as, for example, the race relations and equal opportunities laws. In all matters, the criminal and civil law apply. Some aspects need special vigilance – for example, protection against and prevention of abuse, theft, exploitation and fraud.

Each resident should have a formal agreement (provided by the homeowner or the care manager if the formal contract is held by the social services/work department) setting out the care to be received in the home, the conditions of residence and the fees payable.

### 2.2.10 Sustaining relationships with relatives and friends

A good home values the role which relatives and friends can continue to play in the lives of residents. Their participation should be encouraged wherever residents wish it and their contribution recognised as an important part of the residents' care.

### 2.2.11 Opportunities for leisure activities

Provision for leisure activities in and, where appropriate, outside the home is essential. This should be sensitive to individual tastes and capacities and flexible enough to match them. Resources existing in the neighbourhood should be engaged to help meet the needs of residents. The quality of life in a home will be enhanced by inclusion of the widest possible range of normal activities, particularly those with which residents have been familiar in the past. It should include opportunities to go on outings, to go shopping, and attend places of worship if it is within the individual's capacity to do so.

## 2.3 High standards of care

Individuals must receive the level of care which their own situation requires. It should meet high standards and satisfy the full range of physical, clinical, personal, social, spiritual and emotional needs of the individual.

### 2.3.1 Necessary care

Care and treatment should be provided only if it will be positively beneficial. Care should not mean unnecessary restraint. Treatment (the administration of certain drugs, for example) must never be given for the convenience of the home. Residents should have ready access to appropriate care given by an appropriate person from within or outside the home. It should always be provided with respect for the individual's privacy and dignity.

### 2.3.2 Continuity of care

Wherever possible, and whatever the resident's declining state of health or financial position, continuity of care should be assured. Residents should not have to move out of the home to receive additional care (unless dictated by their medical needs). If possible, it should be brought into the home by external services. Residents should never have to be moved because of financial disputes between funding agencies. Where a home cannot provide all necessary care, or is not intended to (as in the case of respite care), transitions between the home and the person's own home, or the home and a hospice or hospital should be as smooth as possible.

### 2.3.3 Care which is open to scrutiny

Residents (and their relatives or advocates) should be able to complain about the care they receive without fear of being victimised or being asked to leave.

# Entering care

## 3.1    Introduction

People move into continuing care in a variety of circumstances but for each person it is a major life event. Wherever possible, it should be the result of an individual's own informed decision but this may not always be the case. Some will come direct from hospital because a decision to discharge the patient into a supported environment where care is available has been made on the basis of multidisciplinary assessment. Some may come in as the result of decisions made by their relatives or as a result of a crisis. The clinical and other care needs of individuals will vary substantially. In many cases, residents will have been assessed by their local authority social services/work department in consultation with medical and nursing colleagues as requiring residential or nursing home care and some of them will be paid for wholly or in part by the local authority under the NHS and Community Care Act 1990. Others will be paying for themselves.

A prospective resident is likely to be anxious that the decision is the correct one, however it was arrived at. Coming into a home may mean a move away from a familiar area, away from neighbours and friends. It almost certainly means a move into smaller accommodation and the giving up of many personal possessions. Moving into residential care may be occurring at a time of other significant change in the person's life – of crisis or emergency. That change may be due to the loss of a partner or carer with all the accompanying grief which that will entail. To be moving into care may itself sometimes feel like a bereavement.

## 3.2    Choice

Individuals should make their own informed decision to come into care. However, if they themselves cannot make the decision, then those with authority to do so must ensure that the best choice is made on their behalf. Other non-residential options should be considered – for example, packages of care organised after local authority assessment by a care manager which enable both health and social care services to be delivered in the individual's own home.

### 3.2.1    Making the decision

People contemplating entering care should have the opportunity to explore the advantages and disadvantages. A sympathetic and knowledgeable person such as an advocate, social worker or older people's health visitor may be appropriate especially if they have no relative or friend to offer advice. Relevant questions to ask will be:

- why is life difficult?
- why is care needed?
- are there any particular worries and anxieties?
- are these to do with housing, health, disability or other crisis?
- what are the preferred options?
- have any been tried?
- what other circumstances are affecting the situation (for example, are relatives involved and if so are they trying to influence the individual)?

All people have the right to an assessment of their needs by the local authority social services/work department and this should form part of the decision-making process. Under the Carers (Recognition and Services) Act 1995, their carers also have the right to be assessed by the local authority.


## 3.3    Reasons for moving into continuing care

The reasons for deciding to move into care may be varied. Some people may feel they have no other option because of their current circumstances. Some may be faced with the decision suddenly; others may have planned the move for some time.

It may be a combination of several of the following:

- deteriorating mental or physical health;
- general frailty or increasing disability;
- a specific incident such as a fall or illness and hospital admission;
- inability, or fear of being unable, to cope with living at home;
- wanting to be looked after;
- feelings of isolation and loneliness;
- fear of crime;
- fear of falling and not being found;
- bereavement;
- desire for companionship;
- enjoyment of living in a group;
- wish for more convenient accommodation;
- membership of a group or organisation;
- poor housing;
- inability to manage a large house and garden.

The reasons why people come into continuing care have changed in recent years. More are coming in because of failing health and increased dependency than for social reasons. This has consequences for the levels of care required in homes. Managers and staff will need to bear in mind the varying reasons why, and in what circumstances, residents have come into care. Some individuals may need more support than others in coming to terms with the major change in their lives and the home should be sensitive to this. In all circumstances, however, new residents should be made welcome and supported through the period of adjustment which all will experience as newcomers.

## 3.4 Assessment prior to care

Increasingly people moving into care come via the route of a social services-led assessment under the NHS and Community Care Act 1990. They may have been the subject of a joint assessment between social services and the health service prior to hospital discharge. The social services/work department may also have instituted an assessment of their needs while they were still living in their own homes. There will also be an assessment of their financial means.

The assessment of needs should cover a wide range of topics so that an appropriate home can be identified and, once the person has moved in, a comprehensive care plan drawn up. Topics to be covered in the assessment should include:

- the wishes of the older person;
- problems and difficulties as seen by the older person;
- general and specific health problems and any current medication;
- mental health problems;
- social concerns;
- living situation and any housing problems;
- any financial worries;
- pattern of daily life and activities;
- mobility and sensory functioning;
- difficulties in carrying out activities of daily living – for example, dressing, cooking;
- eating, going to the toilet;
- position of carers and relatives;
- medical assessment;
- nursing assessment;
- PAM (professions allied to medicine) assessment.

Copies of the assessment should be given to the home as part of the admission process and form the first stage of care planning. Wherever possible, this should begin before the person moves into the home. Planning should start as early as possible.

## 3.5 Preparation

People planning to enter residential or nursing home care should be able to visit the home and, ideally, stay for several days. Similarly, it is desirable if so wished that the manager of the home should visit potential residents to establish a personal relationship, gain information about their way of life and advise them about what possessions can be taken with them into the home. Many people may be too frail to visit homes in person. One way of overcoming this problem may be for homeowners to arrange for a video to be made (this does not need to be made professionally). This can then be taken (with video player) and shown to potential residents.

### 3.5.1 Sources of advice

There are a number of organisations which can offer advice to people thinking of entering care. Information about them should be made available by social services/work departments, at GP surgeries, clinics, citizens advice bureaux, community health councils (England and Wales), local health councils and councils of social service (Scotland), health and social services councils (Northern Ireland) and other advice agencies (*see Appendix 3 for further details*).

## 3.6 Information

The right decision can only be made if people are properly informed. Under the Registered Homes Act 1984, all homes must make available a brochure or prospectus which sets out the aims and objectives of the home, including the type of resident catered for (for example, those with mental health needs or nursing care needs) and the category of registration (residential, nursing, single, dual), the degree of care offered, the extent to which illness or disability can be accommodated and any restrictions relating to age, gender, group affiliation or religion. In detail, the information should cover the following topics:

- a general description of the home, perhaps with photographs as long as they are realistic;
- details of location and accessibility by public transport (for residents and visitors);
- numbers of residents and living arrangements (for example, small group living);
- availability of single rooms (and double rooms for residents who want them);
- the type of care provided;
- arrangements with local services (hospital consultants, GPs, community health services, voluntary organisations);
- numbers and categories of staff, including nurses in the case of nursing homes;
- food and dining arrangements;
- smoking/non-smoking policy;
- activities (entertainments, religious services, craft activities, outings);

- extent of private space and scope for autonomy within the group environment;
- statement of fees and terms and conditions of residence;
- availability (or not) of trial periods;
- restrictions relating to age, gender, group or religious affiliation;
- conditions under which a resident may be expected to leave;
- category of registration.

It should also be considered good practice to make clear the ownership of the home.

## 3.7 Terms and conditions

A clear statement of the terms and conditions of residence should be given in writing to the resident before moving in. They may be included in the brochure or drawn up separately. The statement should include:

- the level of fees, time and method of payment;
- the services covered by the fees;
- extra services which are charged for separately (these should not include any essential services);
- procedure for increasing fees (including consultation and any right of appeal) when this is necessary;
- the personal items which the resident will be expected or is able to provide for himself or herself;
- the terms under which a resident can vacate the accommodation temporarily;
- the circumstances in which a resident might be asked to leave;
- the procedure under which the resident might be asked to leave;
- the procedure on either side for terminating the agreement or giving notice of changes;
- a statement of insurance cover of the home and where responsibility lies for insuring personal valuables (amounts of cover for residents' property should be made clear and details of insurers given);
- a statement to the effect that the home is registered as a residential care home (or has dual registration) or nursing home by the local authority or health authority which are responsible for seeing that standards are maintained;

- the procedure for making complaints to the owner and information on how to contact the registration authority in the case of unresolved complaints which fall within the scope of the Registered Homes Act 1984;
- procedure on the death of a resident;
- information regarding the home's policy on pets.

## 3.8 Appropriateness

The first two months, or longer, should be mutually recognised as a trial period to allow time to see how well the new resident settles in. Many people will come into care as the result of a crisis or direct from a period in hospital. Relatives or others concerned with their welfare should be made aware of the nature of the trial period. Residents coming from their own homes should be careful to delay selling their houses or terminating their tenancies until they are certain they want to remain in residential care. (This statement is made in the full recognition that for many people there will be considerable pressure placed on them to sell their properties in order to meet accommodation fees. Such pressure does not assist informed and appropriate decision-making.)

### 3.8.1 Reviews

After a trial period, the suitability of the arrangements should be discussed fully with the resident and whoever is the individual's key supporter (relative, friend, care manager, key worker). The possibility of transfer if the arrangement is turning out to be unsuitable should be considered. Review decisions should be recorded and implemented.

Once the individual has become an established resident, a programme of regular reviews to monitor progress and to ensure the resident is satisfied with the home should be agreed and their purpose explained. These reviews will become part of the care plan.

### 3.8.2 Short-term stays

It is generally assumed that once individuals enter a home, they will not return to their own homes. This is not, however, always the case. A short stay may be planned for convalescence, rehabilitation or respite. In other cases, some people's health may improve so that they are able to return home. Appropriate treatment and rehabilitative services should be arranged to ensure that maximum recovery takes place and that the condition of residents does not deteriorate. The aim of rehabilitation (which should be available to all residents) is to retrieve a person's functioning and to maintain it at its highest level.

## 3.9 Funding for individuals coming into residential and nursing home care

### 3.9.1 By the social services department (social work department, health and social services board)

Older people who qualify for statutory funding retain the right to choose which home they would like to live in even though the social services department in England and Wales (social work department in Scotland, health and social services board in Northern Ireland) is wholly or partly funding their care. The department will put an upper limit on the level of fees it is prepared to pay, but it must be sufficient to fund a home able to provide the services required by the resident. If the resident wishes to go into a home with a higher fee level this is still possible provided that the difference is guaranteed (usually by a relative or another organisation).

### 3.9.2 By district health authorities in England and Wales (health boards, health and social services board)

Health authorities, and boards in Scotland and Northern Ireland, will be involved if someone is entering nursing home care from hospital. They may also be wholly or partly funding it if there is a specific medical need. Eligibility criteria agreed by all statutory parties will determine the level of involvement and financial support to be provided. Good hospital discharge arrangements should be in place to ensure a smooth transition from hospital to the home. This includes the prompt transfer of information about any treatment plans or medication. In the case of some patients discharged from psychiatric in-patient care, the 'care programme approach' (special arrangements for someone coming out of psychiatric in-patient care) will have to be observed. Once in the home, continuing professional support should be available if necessary, for example from consultants and physiotherapists. Most trusts and social services/work departments or boards have agreed protocols with each other and local residential and nursing homes about discharge procedures. These should always be observed.

### 3.9.3 Support for residents paying their own fees

Where individuals are paying full fees themselves and are likely to continue to do so throughout their residence, it is not necessary for the statutory services to be involved. However, in these situations it is important that (potential) residents receive similar help to make fully informed and considered decisions and social services/work departments should provide it. This will also be available through independent organisations which specialise in helping people find suitable residential care, through welfare organisations or advice agencies. Care homes associations some-times provide this service.

Homeowners should make clear, before admission, what their policy is when self-financing residents run out of resources. Prospective residents should also make clear their own financial position.

## 3.10 Good practice

As a matter of good practice the process of entering care should:
- be the preferred option after considering alternatives (especially additional help at home);
- be sensitively carried out and be unhurried;
- take account of the person's wishes and lifestyle.

The homeowner or manager should:
- confirm that the home is able to provide the care needed by the person;
- provide full details of conditions, fees, and services provided;
- ask the new resident how he or she wishes to be looked after;
- record sufficient information to enable the home to carry out its responsibilities in caring for the resident;
- develop a care plan detailing the care required and to be provided and by whom;
- have clear arrangements about the roles family and friends may continue to have in the care and life of the resident.

Prospective residents should:
- be helped to find the best place to live;
- not be forced into care against their will;
- not be deceived or misled into entering care.

# Life in the home

## 4.1 Putting principles into practice

The principles which should govern life within the home focus on the importance of promoting residents' independence through enabling them to make their own decisions, fostering their individuality, sustaining family and community contacts and ensuring that they are satisfied with the quality of life and care in the home.

### 4.1.1 Control and independence

Quality of life for individuals will be enhanced if they are able to have control over what happens to them. There is a danger that living in a group means people lose control over their own lives because they are all treated alike and have little privacy or opportunity to be regarded as individuals. It is obvious that in some cases the degree of dependency experienced by many of the residents will preclude any possibility of extensive independence. However, the spirit of the principles of control and independence should govern the care provided to all residents.

*Rules and routines*
The imposition of rules and routines often leads to an erosion of residents' independence. They should therefore be kept to a minimum and employed only to promote rehabilitation (with the agreement of the resident), fulfil statutory requirements, prevent undue disturbance to other residents or ensure acceptable standards of safety and hygiene.

*Risk-taking*
Responsible risk-taking should be regarded as part of the normal expression of people's independence. After appropriate assessment of risk, they should not be discouraged or unduly restrained from undertaking certain activities solely for fear of the consequences, for example that they may hurt themselves. Excessive paternalism and concern for safety may

lead to infringement of personal rights. Those who are competent to judge the risk themselves should be free to make their own decisions so long as they do not threaten the safety and lifestyle of others. Managers should distinguish between behaviour which endangers or seriously inconveniences others and that which involves only the individual concerned. The latter, such as bathing unassisted, or going out unaccompanied, should be restricted only if the resident is not capable of making an informed decision for which he or she can be responsible or if it runs counter to an existing agreed therapy or treatment programme. Managers will need to recognise the demands which getting the balance right place on junior staff and provide support and training to assist them.

### 4.1.2 Individuality

A home where staff recognise the individuality of each of its residents is likely to be a good home. From this recognition is likely to flow a style of management which enables residents to make decisions for themselves, choose the way in which they spend their time, build friendships with whom they wish, and find satisfaction in living in the home environment.

*Ways of maintaining individuality*
Ensuring that residents have their own private space, with plenty of reminders about their identity for people with dementia, is an essential part of maintaining their individuality. Single rooms, places to withdraw to from busy, active communal areas, opportunities to prepare food and drink for themselves, and choice over when they get up and go to bed will all contribute to the process.

*A resident's earlier life*
It is easy to underestimate and undervalue the qualities, experiences and talents of people in care. Residents' willingness to share their past experiences, interests and life histories with their companions will help create their individual identity for fellow residents and staff. A reciprocal regard for family and friends and an encouragement of their involvement with the continued care of the resident and in the life of the group (with the residents' agreement) will reinforce the esteem in which residents are held.

*Culture, background and ethnicity*

The principle of valuing individual identity means that anyone, from any background, should be treated as unique. As people grow older, their earlier associations and allegiances will remain important (and often become more so). People moving into residential care are likely to want to go into homes which reflect their particular ethnic, religious, educational, occupational or social backgrounds. Where this has not been possible, and they are living in a mixed setting, their particular needs, be they cultural, religious, language or any other, should be recognised and accommodated. Wherever possible, the staff complement should reflect the cultural and ethnic mix of residents in the home.

### 4.1.3 Satisfaction with the quality of daily life

A key measure of the quality of life in a home will be the degree to which residents are satisfied in their daily lives. This will relate to:

- the activities of daily life;
- the quality of food and the way in which it is served;
- opportunities, for those who wish, to engage in social and leisure activities;
- quality of care;
- choice in daily routines;
- the skills and attitudes of staff, managers and volunteers.

Residents should be able to look forward positively to the day, and days, ahead. The regular testing of residents' views about the quality of the service they receive should be part of the management process. For people with dementia this may be done by using techniques such as 'dementia care mapping' which involves careful observation of individuals over a specific period of time and assessment of their interaction and reactions. Managers should also be receptive to the ideas and suggestions that residents, their family, friends and advocates might make to improve the general quality of life in the home. Many relatives and friends are sometimes fearful of appearing critical lest it rebound on their relative. They are also often very grateful for the care given and feel guilty they can no longer provide this at home, so they do not want to criticise. Therefore a home has to generate a positive and easy welcome for ideas if it wishes to hear them. Openness and receptivity should be seen as a mark of good management and procedures should be established for enabling this.

## 4.2　Daily life

Domestic routines are necessary for the smooth running of a home and are part of the normal rhythm of most people's days in any setting. They need to take account of individual needs and preferences. As far as possible, routines should be agreed with residents and carried out in a friendly and flexible way.

*Examples of flexibility:*
- changing the time of a regular bath so that the care assistant can take the resident for a shopping trip;
- a resident having a meal at a later time in the afternoon (instead of the meal at lunchtime) so that he or she can go to an education class in the morning;
- raising plants in the corner of the conservatory because there is no greenhouse;
- a resident with dementia who has always worked a night shift being able to sleep all day and be active at night.

*Examples of unacceptable practice:*
- early rising for the convenience of staff;
- routinely arranging chairs around the edge of the room and leaving the television on with no one watching;
- serving the same meal with no choice to everyone at the same time;
- serving the last meal of the day to suit the cook's working hours;
- adhering to rigid bath routines.

### 4.2.1　Getting up and going to bed

One measure of a flexible approach to daily life is the extent to which residents are able to choose when they get up and when they go to bed. It should always be their choice and never be fixed to fit into a routine dictated by staff rotas. Some people with dementia lose their sense of night and day. In these cases, assistance may include reviewing medication, the provision of highly visible clocks and orientation to daylight and darkness.

### 4.2.2　Mealtimes and food

Food and mealtimes are of great social importance in the lives of all people. This applies to the residential setting as much as anywhere else. Being separated from the sights, smells and noise of cooking food is seen by some as a deprivation. Involvement in the process of preparing food is regarded by others as an essential part of life, although it can be a welcome relief that meals are provided. The degree to which people are directly involved in preparing and serving food and participating fully in mealtimes will depend on their abilities and legal restrictions but where possible the emphasis should be on willing participation (as long as this does not mean residents are standing in for staff).

The following points should be observed:

- people should have the opportunity, if they wish and if they are able, to prepare snacks and drinks for themselves. This might mean kettles in rooms (if this has been assessed as an acceptable risk) or small kitchen facilities near or in their own accommodation;
- residents, according to their capacities, should have the opportunity to be involved in menu planning, preparation, laying tables, clearing away and washing up. Staff should make great efforts to find out individual preferences for types of food and style of preparation, particularly where residents are less able to do things for themselves;
- residents should have regular opportunities to talk to the cook(s) and catering staff about the sort of food they like and to comment on the meals they are given;
- assistance with eating food should be given individually and discreetly and with care and sensitivity. Staff should *sit* with the person they are assisting. Residents should always have a choice of food so that they can avoid the type of food which they find difficult to handle (for example, peas) or, for people who find mealtimes too stressful, buffet-style meals might be an alternative. If people wish to eat in private in their own rooms they should be enabled to do so. Care should be taken by staff to enable residents to make their views known if another resident's messy eating habits cause distress to others;
- food preferences based on ethnic, religious and ethical observances should be respected. Storage and preparation facilities may be required, and staff may need to be trained in how to prepare some sorts of food and to find out what residents want;

- food should be nutritious, well-balanced and appealing. Great efforts should be made to ensure that food is offered which residents take pleasure in eating;
- the serving of food should be seen as part of the social life of the home. Preplated food as a general way of serving meals is unacceptable because it denies this. Plastic tableware should not be used. Care should be taken to ensure that food offered to an individual resident is attractive even though it has to be appropriately prepared to meet the physical capacity of the individual. Food should only be liquidised if absolutely necessary and care should be taken to present it attractively (for example, by keeping different types and colours of food separate);
- dining rooms should not have the appearance of institutional canteens. Furniture and furnishings should be domestic in style. Chairs should be of a comfortable height with sturdy arms (but which can be pulled right up to the table) to assist those who have difficulty in getting up from sitting. Residents should be able to choose how mealtimes are organised and how dining tables are arranged. Choice of sitting at tables alone or with one or two or several other people should be possible. Regimentation at mealtimes – all people being required to sit down to the meal at the same time – should be avoided unless it is the clear wish of residents to do so;
- dining rooms should be non-smoking although smoking areas may be designated elsewhere as long as this is in line with the home's overall smoking policy;
- expert advice from dieticians can be sought and followed with regard to nutritional requirements. Special diets specified on medical grounds must be adhered to;
- the handling, storage, preparation and serving of food must comply with all official requirements.

### 4.2.3 Activities

The therapeutic benefits derived from being physically and mentally active are well known and all homes must provide stimulation of this sort for their residents. The range of opportunities available in the home for people to pursue leisure and intellectual activities should reflect the diversity of its residents and their social and cultural interests and intellectual and physical capacities. It is important for staff to remember that just because people have become infirm and just because they have reached old age, it does not mean that they all have the same likes and dislikes. Not everyone wants to sit and watch television (or the same programme on television); not everyone likes playing bingo or having singsongs. Scope for choice and variety should be made available. Residents confined to bed should as far as possible also have the opportunity for social interaction and intellectual stimulation.

- in many cases, involvement with the local community will provide welcome social activity for residents. Children from schools may wish to visit and in some cases entertain residents. Carol singing at Christmas is a good example although contact should not be restricted to festival times. Local voluntary organisations may wish to establish a continuing relationship with the home which residents may welcome. Residents should always be consulted before any arrangements with outside organisations are established;
- residents may wish to maintain their religious links once they have come into care. The home should positively foster such links – with religious and spiritual bodies of all faiths and denominations as appropriate. They may be a source of comfort and reassurance to residents. The wishes of individual residents not to have links of any sort with religious bodies should be respected. Religious belief should not be assumed;
- staff should be sensitive to the changing needs of residents. Over time, some people may wish to withdraw from activities that previously they were closely involved in. These changing attitudes should be picked up and acted upon.

*General examples of daily activities:*

- gatherings in the home, coffee and tea groups;
- exercise classes, movement to music, dancing;
- books, newspapers (including large-print and audiotape);
- indoor and outdoor gardening (with modifications for disabled people);
- craft activities;
- intellectual activity – education classes, quizzes, life history and reminiscence work;

- alternative therapies (aromatherapy, snoezelen room);
- swimming, walking;
- active games (carpet bowls, quoits);
- pets (individuals', the home's, visiting);
- religious worship;
- intergenerational activities (with local schools);
- shopping trips, outings;
- fundraising, social events, local community activities.

For some people, the ability to participate will be limited by restricted movement, deafness, visual impairment or memory loss. When individual residents have a clear wish to participate in certain activities, every effort should be made to help them overcome or compensate for these restrictions by providing personal assistance or aids and adaptations.

In everyday life, many families and friends enjoy doing things together and additional pleasure can be generated for residents and their visitors if opportunities for their involvement exist within the home and on outings. Visiting often increases when people feel that they are coming in to join in an activity or to assist residents.

### 4.2.4 The needs of people with dementia

An organised day is particularly helpful for people with dementia. It stimulates them and builds on the abilities they still retain. The table opposite lists the sorts of activities which may be possible and sets out the benefits to be derived.

### 4.2.5 Special occasions

Special occasions are important for both the communal life of the home and for the individual. Residents' birthdays should be celebrated if they wish; the opportunity to have a party or meal for invited guests from outside and within the home emphasises the individuality of residents. Other individual celebrations which can be shared with the group include anniversaries, a grandchild's marriage and birth of great-grandchildren. The death of a resident should be marked in an appropriate way (*see Chapter 10*).

There are many religious and cultural festivals and occasions that may be observed and celebrated. The exact range will depend on the cultural background, beliefs and interests of the residents. Where there is a mix of people living in the home, it may be appropriate to consult and involve a range of local religious and community leaders.

| Type of activity | Purpose and benefit |
|---|---|
| • shared coffee time<br>• reading newspapers<br>• TV and radio (serials) | • awareness<br>(being in contact with the world) |
| • music and movement<br>• exercise classes<br>• games<br>• singing | • physical exercise<br>(maintains muscle strength and<br>improves coordination skills) |
| • reminiscence sessions<br>• quizzes<br>• reminders of events<br>• news-sheets<br>• board games | • mental stimulation<br>(helps retain short-term memory) |
| • dressing<br>• laying tables and washing up<br>• cooking<br>• cleaning<br>• gardening | • taking part in daily life<br>(feel needed and useful) |
| • arts and crafts | • being creative<br>(may provide new skills or learn new skills) |
| • sharing activities with other people<br>• links with families and friends<br>• links with local community | • having an interest in life<br>(develops meaning and confidence) |
| • familiar chores such as dusting, laundry<br>• longstanding hobbies<br>• activities related to past work experience | • maintaining skills and confidence |
| • encourage smiles and laughter<br>• relaxation therapies<br>• music and songs<br>• close relationships with staff who listen | • expressing emotions<br>(relieves tension and stress) |

## 4.3    Clothes

A person's sense of identity is partly linked to his or her appearance. Clothes may be an important part of this. All residents should wear their own identifiable clothes and the staff should take care to ensure that clothes do not go astray or get damaged by careless handling. The practice of supplying clothes from a communal pool is never acceptable. Residents (and family and friends) should be advised about the suitability of fabrics for laundering when planning to purchase new clothes. Staff should be ready to assist in making arrangements to purchase new clothes. The following points need to be observed:

- all personal belongings of residents should be treated with care;
- clothes should be labelled discreetly with name tags to ensure they do not get lost during laundering;
- clothes should be kept fresh and clean. Residents should be able to get involved in washing and hanging out laundry, ironing and mending if they wish, as long as this complies with the law and regulations;
- opportunities for handwashing and ironing should be available and staff should check regularly whether clothes need mending. Clothes should be drycleaned if necessary. If additional charges are made for all or some of these services, this should be made clear in the terms and conditions of residence;
- where residents have difficulty in dressing, for example because of arthritis or rheumatism, it may be necessary to choose clothes which are easy to put on or have simple fastenings. Clothes which are easy to remove may help people who suffer from incontinence. Occupational therapists can offer advice. There may also be benefits in using thermal or other special fabrics.

## 4.4    Personal care

Many residents will need assistance with personal care – washing, dressing, eating, going to the toilet and getting about (either walking or in a wheelchair) – in order to be able to participate in the social life of the home. Any tasks associated with providing care of this sort should be undertaken with due regard to the privacy and dignity of the individual.

In particular:
- attention should be paid to ensuring such things as catheters and colostomy bags are not exposed;
- special care should be taken of dentures, spectacles and hearing aids;
- residents should choose when they are washed or bathed and they should be assisted in doing as much for themselves as they wish. While encouragement to bath regularly should be given, rigid bath routines should be avoided.

## 4.5 Terms of address

It is important to take account of individual preferences in the way in which people are addressed. A person is entitled to be called whatever he or she wishes whether it be, for example, Mrs Brown, Alice Brown or Alice. Names and special names are not only labels of identity, they are personal possessions to be handled in the manner their owners choose. It is reasonable to wish to be addressed in different ways by different people. Even when people invite fellow residents to use their first or special names, they may still prefer strangers or members of staff to use a more formal mode of address.

Staff should never use terms of address which patronise residents or make them seem like children. They should not discuss residents' personal matters in the hearing of other residents. They should not talk to each other over the head of a resident as if he or she were an inanimate object.

## 4.6 Personal relationships

Residents should have opportunities for emotional, physical and sexual expression and for intimate and personal relationships within and outside the home as they wish. Sensitivity will always be required to prevent possible exploitation of vulnerable individuals. The ability to manage relationships and to assume personal responsibility may fluctuate over time. Nevertheless residents will continue to have the same needs as other people for expressive behaviour and physical human contact and these needs should be respected.

## 4.7 Pets

Many older people value contact with pets and will have had pets living with them until the time of moving into the home. The following points should be taken into account:

- homes should make clear in their information brochures whether or not pets can be brought with residents when they come to live in the home;
- it is important to recognise the therapeutic benefits of pets (for some people) in deciding what policy will operate in the home;
- if individual residents are not able to have their own pets it may be possible for the home to keep pets which belong to the home as a whole or to have them visit;
- there are national and local schemes which can arrange for visiting pets.

## 4.8 Transport

Having access to transport will improve the quality of many residents' lives. Some homes may be able to run their own minibus. Other options may be:

- borrowing or hiring an adapted minibus;
- dial-a-ride schemes;
- car schemes (hospital transport);
- volunteers' and staff cars;
- taxis;
- local buses (with agreements to stop outside the home);
- electric outdoor wheelchairs or battery cars (for loan to residents).

Anyone driving a vehicle should have the necessary qualifications and all formal requirements must be met (insurance, minibus regulations, driver training and certification, seatbelts, wheelchair clamps). Any signwriting on vehicles should be discreet and not draw attention to the residents unnecessarily or in a stigmatising way.

## 4.9 The role of staff, relatives and friends, advocates and volunteers

The way in which staff, relatives, friends and other supporters are involved with residents on a day-to-day basis will affect residents' well-being and sense of satisfaction.

### 4.9.1 Staff

Staff have a responsibility to be alert to the needs of residents. They should be ready to talk and listen to them during the course of the day and especially at night. Some residents may find it hard to express their true feelings about how they are and what they want to do. Staff may be best placed to discover some of these things while going about their general duties. They should be sympathetic and sensitive to the residents to enable them to express their feelings.

A normal and natural part of daily conversation for staff should be to talk about what residents would like to do or have, about ideas for doing different things, or changes they would like made.

Management should ensure that opportunities are built into the staff routine so that time can be devoted to doing things with individual residents or to talking to them (especially about things which might be worrying them). The trust and friendship of a key worker or other staff member is particularly important. The value of such time is demonstrated by residents often saying they appreciate their bath because it is the only time they receive individual attention from a staff member; likewise staff report that this is when residents often talk most about personal matters. Bathtime should not be the only occasion for this.

### 4.9.2 Relatives and friends

Relatives and friends have an important role to play within homes. They should be encouraged to participate in the daily life of the home as long as the resident wants them to. This might involve sharing meals, doing shopping, washing hair, reading and other social activities. Some homes may wish to draw up agreements or contracts with relatives and friends, setting out what each party might be expected to do or provide. Having relatives actively involved in the home is likely to act as a check on possible abusive behaviour by staff.

While the benefits of involving relatives and friends are usually clear, it should also be recognised that relationships between them and the resident may not always be harmonious. Staff should be careful not to make unwarranted value judgements but always be ready to support the resident in whatever way is appropriate should the resident so wish.

### 4.9.3 The role of advocates

Many people living in homes have no relatives or friends to take an interest in them or provide advice and support in matters affecting their daily lives. Volunteer advocates should be welcomed by the home to provide support to residents if residents so wish. There are different sorts of advocates – from those who provide a steady source of support and friendship to those who act on behalf of people who 'lack capacity' (a legal term). Local advocacy groups have been set up in many areas and can give information to residents and home managers and staff about what they can offer.

### 4.9.4 The role of volunteers

Volunteers from the local community may wish to become involved in the life of the home and may be suited to act in a 'befriending' role as well as undertaking more social and communal activities (for example, leading reminiscence work or exercise classes). Where residents want this, then it should be encouraged. Care should be taken, however, that residents do not feel their private space (their home) has been 'invaded' by outsiders although many residents will greatly value continuing links with the local community. Volunteers should not be used as unpaid staff. It may be helpful for the home to provide leaflets for potential volunteers setting out their roles and responsibilities when they are helping in the home.

The other key role volunteers play in homes and other organisations in the voluntary sector is that of trustees – taking overall legal responsibility for the policy and standards of the establishments under their governance. Under both charity and company law such trusteeship is central in ensuring good practice.

## 4.10 Communication in the home

Residents need to be kept informed about what is happening in the home if they are to be able to participate fully. Staff should ensure that they keep residents informed directly. Additionally, in some larger establishments, noticeboards and news-sheets may be useful ways of ensuring that residents know what is going on in the home. Reliance on non-personal means of communication should not be a substitute for direct communication between staff and residents as part of normal social interaction.

## 4.11 Group meetings or committees

It is important that residents (and their family and friends) have an opportunity to have a say in how the home is organised and run. Residents' groups, relatives' groups, groups of friends, are all ways of facilitating this. However, if formal residents' meetings are held, they may well fail in some cases because they are seen as artificial exercises. Informal, natural, day-to-day conversations, for example over meals, at coffee time or on social occasions, may be more productive. Nevertheless, formal meetings and regular gatherings of residents can be held to discuss issues of importance. Staff and managers should be aware of, and compensate for, the difficulty some people may have in hearing what is said or in participating in large meetings. The existence of a formal residents' meeting may be regarded by inspectors as an indicator of residents' involvement.

# Care

## 5.1    Introduction

Moving into care is often accompanied by negative feelings and a sense of loss of status. This needs to be understood and taken into account by those providing care, to minimise as far as possible the loss of self-confidence and the failing sense of self-worth. Receiving intimate care in a new setting, often away from loved ones, especially at a time of adjusting to the 'home' as home, may be particularly difficult. Some people may resent their increased dependency, the need to receive care in a new and different environment and their reliance on staff. Their sense of loss may be similar to a feeling of bereavement. Staff sensitivity to these feelings will be required in order to enable residents to come to terms with their changing needs. For people with dementia, with impaired memory and reasoning, the transition may be bewildering.

Living in a home in no way diminishes residents' rights of access to health and rehabilitative services available in the community. This includes the right to choose their own GP and to see him or her in private. Managers, with the consent of the resident, should be kept informed of any necessary changes in the resident's care. In the case of residential care homes, the rights of residents to have access to community nursing services does not in any way put at risk the registration of the home as a residential care home. Managers have a right of access to available community resources and advice in the interests of their residents.

## 5.2 Principles of care

The care which is provided within the home should be tailored to meet the needs (social, personal, nursing or medical) of each individual. It should be provided on the basis of an assessment which is both timely and comprehensive. At all times it should be provided with respect in a manner which is sensitive, maintaining the dignity of whoever is receiving care. The privacy of individuals, particularly in all matters dealing with intimate care-giving, should be ensured at all times and their cultural and gender needs and sensitivities should always be recognised.

Care should be given by, or supervised by, skilled (professionally qualified where necessary) and trained people; training opportunities should be provided for staff at all levels who should be encouraged to take them up. The importance of early recognition of symptoms – particularly mental health problems (for example, depression and dementia) – cannot be over-emphasised. The first essential is to try to ensure that the causes of any symptoms are diagnosed and any necessary treatment given. Many kinds of physical illness can give rise to an acute confusional state, as can over-sedation or other inappropriate medication. Dementia is the condition which generally gives cause for most concern but depressive illness is very common in old age and can be mistaken for dementia. Delusional symptoms can develop in an otherwise intact personality. All these conditions can be cured or at least alleviated and it is essential that managers take responsibility for seeing that no such illness is ignored. Junior staff should be trained to recognise symptoms as they appear. The importance of calling in outside expertise via the GP should also be recognised.

Care-giving should never be coercive, and should always guard against abuse and restraint. Nothing should be done which makes individuals lose their self-esteem. Even at their most frail and vulnerable, individuals should be helped to make choices about the care they receive.

## 5.3 The continuum of care

The Registered Homes Act 1984 makes a distinction between residential care homes (in Part I) and nursing homes (in Part II). Under the Act, residential care homes provide accommodation and personal care while nursing homes provide care which requires the skills of, or supervision by, a registered nurse. In practice the differences are sometimes hard to define, particularly because of the changing needs which an individual may experience while remaining in the same setting. Dual registration with the local authority and the health authority overcomes some of the legal problems but it is acknowledged that some flexibility is required to take account of fluctuations in residents' health. The registration authorities will need to review the position periodically to determine whether changes in registration are required. In residential care homes, any nursing care provided must be under the control of a community nurse with an agreed protocol relating to named individuals within the home.

### 5.3.1  Types of care

Care should be provided holistically – that is, looking at the whole needs of residents as individuals and not isolating different elements of care into separate unrelated tasks. However, for the purposes of this code it is useful to identify different elements to help clarify roles and responsibilities.

*Social support*

Social support within the home is the support which is provided to older people to enable them to function as social beings. It includes social activities designed to enhance residents' sense of well-being, moral support, care and attention paid to ensure individuals can maintain contact with family and friends in the community, and making advice and advocacy available to help individuals deal with their personal, financial and legal affairs if desired. Attention to the spiritual needs of individuals is also important and care should be taken to identify what those needs may be for particular individuals.

The provision of social support is an integral part of many of the daily activities of the home. It forms an element in getting up, eating and drinking, being involved in social activities within the home, having spiritual needs attended to, getting around the building and garden, and going to bed. Other sections in this code deal with these aspects in more detail. Staff should be alert to the needs of residents and should spend time listening to their views on what sort of activities they may wish to become involved in or stay away from.

*Personal care*

Personal care is the intimate tending of physical needs, which the individual finds difficult or impossible to do alone. Some sorts of personal care will be given during the normal pattern of daily life – helping a resident to get around, helping at mealtimes. Other aspects will require privacy and sensitivity – washing and bathing, going to the toilet, nail-cutting. The individual should always be able to choose where and when these activities are performed – they should not be the subject of rigid routines. Equipment which is used should be personal to the individual (flannels, soap, scissors).

*Nursing care*

Nursing care encompasses both social and personal care but qualified nurses who provide or supervise the provision of care also offer distinct knowledge and skills which derive from their professional education and experience. They can thus help to balance the health or clinical needs of older people in care with their daily activities and aspirations.

Many of the functions categorised as nursing care are also carried out by other care staff under the supervision of a qualified nurse within the nursing home, or in a residential care home under the supervision of a community nurse or the resident's GP (as would be the case if the resident were still living in his or her own home).

The holistic approach which modern nursing adopts looks to the needs of the whole individual. Following assessment of care needs, nurses may work closely with individual residents, or supervise care delivered by others. Nursing involvement is essential for the overall assessment, monitoring and coordination of health care.

The care component of a home should be structured to include all or some of the following and will be undertaken by a nurse, or by a care worker under the supervision, where appropriate, of a nurse:
- assessment;
- formulation of a care plan;
- allocating responsibility to a particular nurse (primary nurse, key worker);
- monitoring and observing;
- coordination of care by others;
- health and illness recognition;
- prevention of complications;

- physical and emotional comfort;
- pain control;
- liaison with doctors, specialist nurses and professions allied to medicine outside the home;
- rehabilitation, including maintenance rehabilitation;
- intimate personal care;
- recognition of social needs;
- mobility;
- disease management;
- supervision of medication;
- prevention and management of pressure sores;
- wound assessment and care;
- continence assessment and management;
- insertion of catheters;
- auditing of standards of care.

As important as these is the need for health promotion and health maintenance within the home on a continuing basis. Advice and help should also be available for oral care, nutrition, sight and hearing. In addition to these is the ability to empathise, to listen, to think creatively and to communicate.

On occasions nurses who have specialist expertise and experience will be required to attend residents who, for example, have cancer, diabetes, a psychiatric illness, challenging behaviour, a stoma or who are dying. Agreements and protocols with local trusts will ensure the availability of nurses in these situations.

*Medical care*
Medical care may be required on a regular or intermittent basis, either from a GP or specialist consultant after referral by a GP, depending on specific medical needs. Close links with GPs are essential. Residents should retain their own GPs if they wish, and they are willing, without feeling pressure to register with a local one who acts as the home's overall GP. However, in some cases, where the person's GP does not want to continue looking after the patient after entry into a home, this may be the only option. Whatever arrangement is arrived at it is important that GPs involved in providing medical care and advice to residents have some extra experience and proven interest in the care of older people. Where there are difficulties in involving GPs with the home, the local health authority

will need to advise. GPs should be involved in the assessment of patients on admission to a home, and in reviewing their care and medication.

The split between residential and nursing home provision has often meant that different sorts of care have been restricted in each setting. Dual registration may in some cases overcome the problem but sometimes residential care settings have been unable to provide nursing and medical care, although needed, while nursing homes have tended to concentrate too little on providing social care. It also means in some instances that residents in nursing homes have had less access to the primary health care team and specialist community nurses than those in residential homes. Bridging the gap is one of the most important objectives for all care providers.

### Relationships with outside health services

Protocols should be drawn up with GPs and local hospital consultants for dealing with discharges from and admissions to hospital, clarifying the roles and responsibilities of all parties and for visiting residents in their accommodation. Staff from the local psychogeriatric service such as the consultant psychiatrist, the psychologist and the community psychiatric nurse (CPN) can be very helpful in planning and reviewing the care and treatment of people with dementia and depression. Local GPs and/or their practice staff and attached staff should be encouraged to lay on health promotion advice and activities for their individual patients and for general availability within the home. Health promotion advisors from the local health authority should also be involved in developing activity programmes for residents.

### Community nursing and specialist nursing care

Where the home does not have qualified nursing staff (that is, in a residential care home or sheltered housing) protocols should be drawn up setting out arrangements for local community nursing services to be available for residents when they need nursing care. Clear lines of communication should be established which are known to all staff about when and how to call in community nursing services. Similar arrangements may need to be established with specialist nursing services (Macmillan and Marie Curie nurses, CPNs, or specialist nurses from the community nursing service – for diabetes, stoma care, for example) which will also be available to nursing homes.

## 5.4 Administration of medication

### 5.4.1 Safety

Staff need to take meticulous care over the administration of drugs. Only nominated and trained staff should be involved in giving medication to residents. Procedures should be put in place to ensure the wrong drug is never administered. Attaching a picture of the individual to the drug chart can be a safeguard against making mistakes. Some conditions, for example diabetes or Parkinson's Disease, require a strict drug routine which may not fit into the daily meal pattern. These routines must be observed.

Medicines must be kept safely, with full records of their receipt, administration and disposal. Medicines should be administered directly to the resident and recorded as taken (or not) and should not be transferred to open unnamed containers for distribution. If the medicine is not taken it should be disposed of and accounted for in line with the registration authority's disposal of drugs policy. The district health authority's pharmaceutical officer will advise.

### 5.4.2 The NAHAT guidelines

The National Association of Health Authorities and Trusts (NAHAT) has produced guidelines for the handling, storage and disposal of drugs as appropriate. Homes should be familiar with these and abide by their requirements as appropriate.

### 5.4.3 The dangers of polypharmacy

A common problem amongst residents is the large number of drugs (polypharmacy) which they are taking, often over a period of years without any proper review. Sometimes this leads to unwanted effects or unnecessary confusion. The use of sedatives and sleeping pills is sometimes prescribed as a matter of course. The problem may be caused by drugs being prescribed from hospital without any proper feedback to the resident's GP and vice versa. It may be eliminated if the GP reviews the medication on admission to the home and reviews it regularly thereafter every two or three months.

### 5.4.4 Non-prescribed remedies

Non-prescribed remedies should be purchased separately by each resident for his or her own use (or someone else should do it on his or her behalf).

Communal supplies of non-prescribed remedies and creams should not be kept. This does not preclude the home from keeping proper first aid supplies, which it must do by law.

Wherever possible, and depending on their capabilities, residents should take responsibility for their own medicines and a monitored dosage system, in which a week's supply is divided up into separate, sealed compartments, may be helpful. A positive decision should be taken as to who (resident or home) is responsible so that no false presumptions are made. The home should have a policy on self-administration of drugs. It should always be remembered that in law homes have a duty of care and managers should be clear under what circumstances GPs will be informed of residents' self-administration.

The district pharmacist is a useful source of advice on any matters to do with medication.

## 5.5   Care plans

Care plans for individual residents, in both nursing homes and residential care homes, are essential to ensure that each resident receives the individual care he or she requires. They are a necessary part of the record-keeping of any home and facilitate good communication between residents and internal and external staff. Residents (and their relatives where appropriate) should take a lead in saying how they would like to be looked after. Care plans should form the basis for daily care and they should be referred to regularly and updated as appropriate. They should be available to relevant staff at all times. Consistency in their implementation is particularly critical in dementia care. Residents should have direct access to them, preferably retaining them themselves where possible. Their permission must be sought for people other than the responsible care staff to see them and use the information they contain. With the individual resident's permission, the care plan may be used by inspectors as one means of checking on the quality of care provided in the home.

### 5.5.1   Drawing up care plans

Care plans should be developed by each home according to its type and the condition of the residents. They are likely to be more complex in nursing homes. The process is a developmental one and includes the following stages:

- assessments covering the major areas of care. If assessments have been made before coming into care, they should form the starting point;
- specific professional assessments including medical and nursing if not already completed should be undertaken and included in the plan. Standard dependency scales may be useful tools for planning and monitoring the care plan (some of these processes will also be carried out in residential care homes);
- deciding with the resident the best way to provide the care. This should include the contribution that relatives are able to make;
- the plan should be monitored and reviewed at prescribed intervals, usually every three to six months. The review should focus on the resident's experience and opinion on what should happen in the future;
- the care should be revised in the light of care plan reviews;
- the plan should be confidential and remain the property of the resident who should have a copy of the plan.

Care plans should be factual and jargon-free.

*Content of care plans*
The following areas should be considered for the care plan although not everything needs to be included for every person:
- basic personal details, date of birth, relatives, next of kin;
- social information (if given by the resident), previous places lived, work, family, interests;
- preferences about daily life;
- food preferences and any dietary requirements (both medical and cultural);
- the part relatives and friends wish to play;
- general health record (including past medical history which affects present functioning);
- risk assessments for safety;
- the extent of confusion or challenging behaviour;
- risk assessments for manual handling;
- risk assessments for pressure sores;
- medications and treatment (and whether the resident is able to look after this personally);
- any nursing care required;

- ability of resident to care for self;
- any help required and preferences as to how this should be given;
- any preferences about future care options;
- religious, spiritual and cultural background;
- expressed wishes in relation to death and dying.

Wherever possible, clear and attainable goals should be set out in the care plan which the resident and care staff can follow on a planned basis, with a timescale (which should not be too far distant) for achievement. In this way progress can be monitored and incentives given to both resident and staff.

Advice about drawing up plans may be sought from the registration authority.

### 5.5.2  Key workers

Depending on the size of the home, it may be considered appropriate to establish key worker arrangements. Key workers take responsibility for individual residents and ensure that 'their' residents are attended to and looked after in accordance with their particular needs (especially as laid down in the care plan). If this approach is not adopted, alternative systems should show that they fulfil the requirements for personal attention. Where a key worker system is in place, residents should be able to have the key worker changed without difficulty or recrimination if they request it.

## 5.6  Care for people with dementia

### 5.6.1  In the case of physical illness or disability

It is important to be alert to signs of physical illness in people with dementia. There is a danger that they may be overlooked. Emotions and intellectual functioning are affected by a person's physical health. This is particularly important for people with dementia because:
- people with dementia cannot always work out that they have a physical illness;
- people with dementia may not know how to communicate their symptoms such as irritation, pain or nausea. Greater use of non-verbal communication skills may be needed in order to understand how they are feeling;

- people with dementia may not take the appropriate action. For example, they may spit food out if their mouths are sore rather than seek treatment.

*Staff responsibilities*
Staff have to be alert to changes in behaviour or to indirect verbal explanations which may indicate that there is a problem. Urinary tract infections, for example, may make someone suddenly more confused, or constipation may make someone shout for help. The possibility of pain should always be considered if there is a change in behaviour. In general, staff should always beware of assuming that people with dementia do not understand. With patience and perseverance, staff will be able to establish relationships of mutual understanding.

Caring for someone with dementia who is physically ill can be problematic in that they may not understand that it is important that they stay in bed or stay inside. More generally, staff have an invaluable role in drawing attention to changes in behaviour which may help the doctor's diagnosis. A knowledge of the person's past can be useful in understanding how they cope, or do not cope, with illness. Relatives too can be helpful in sharing their knowledge and understanding of the resident.

Regular monitoring and review of a resident's condition is essential to ensure that the correct treatment and care is being given.

### 5.6.2 Personal care

As far as possible people with dementia should undertake their own personal care because:
- they will have strong preferences about toileting, washing, dressing and other personal routines;
- it will enhance their confidence and self-esteem;
- it provides purposeful and normal activity to fill the day.

It is always much easier and quicker to help people rather than let them do it for themselves and people with dementia can be very slow indeed. Staff may also have to suppress their own views on, for example, the advantages of a bath over a strip wash favoured by many older people.

The assessment skills of staff are very important. They need to be able to break personal care tasks down into small steps and assess which ones the resident can or cannot do. People with dementia may not be able to dress themselves, for example, because they have forgotten which order clothes go on but if the clothes are placed in the right order they can manage (the right order being, of course, the order they prefer and are used to).

The same careful assessments are needed for all personal care activities. Some people may be able to eat a meal if the right implements are put into their hands, but not otherwise. Another person may be able to use the toilet at night if he or she can see it; so a light needs to be left on. A creative problem-solving approach is required and success can be rewarding for staff and resident alike.

For the individual, much of the experience of dementia is an experience of constant failure. Remaining abilities need to be identified and recognised to enhance confidence and self-esteem. Mealtimes can provide many opportunities to identify and make use of remaining skills even if it is just those of pouring tea out of the teapot. When help has to be given, for example in actually feeding a person, it needs to be as one adult helping another. Time to achieve a rapport and dignity in such a situation is essential. A great many actions which humiliate, diminish and de-skill people with dementia are done because staff are not encouraged to invest time in assisting them or to see the activity as a potentially therapeutic use of time.

Staff can all benefit from an understanding of the way stress impairs everyone. People function less well if they are stressed. Providing an environment where stress factors such as noise are diminished, ensuring that staff are not communicating their own stress in their behaviour and helping in a natural and positive way will all help people struggling to undertake their own physical care. All physical care activities can be made more or less stressful by staff. Being helped to the toilet can be an opportunity for a friendly chat or it can be a stressful experience. Being lifted into a bath on a hoist can be an opportunity for a personal reflection and a shared song or it can be terrifying.

## 5.7 Palliative care

Palliative care should be provided in any continuing care setting whenever it is needed. It should take account of the whole needs of the individual and his or her family and friends. It is important to reassure residents that, should they need it, they will receive an appropriate level of palliative care without having to move out of the home – for example into hospital – unless medically necessary. This means that appropriate care which will provide comfort and relief from pain can be provided by a multi-disciplinary team within the home or brought in as required from outside (for example from Macmillan or Marie Curie nurses or from a local hospice). It is important for GPs to be fully involved.

The doctor (either the consultant or GP) should provide a written plan of treatment to include:

- names of medications (brand names, chemical name and any alternative names);
- purpose and use of each drug;
- dose and timing of regular medication;
- dose for break-through pain (pain which occurs before the next regular dose);
- dose and timing for incident pain (pain associated with movement, change of dressing or other incident);
- strategies and medications for avoiding unwanted effects of medications (typically vomiting, constipation and drowsiness);
- associated physical care, nursing and provision of comfort;
- names and telephone numbers of contacts, especially for problems during the night;
- monitoring of treatment. There should be regular contact with the consultant or GP to assess effectiveness of pain control.

The resident will need to be reassured that measures to control pain will be adequate and available should the time come when it is required. In addition, staff should be aware of the differing attitudes and meanings attached to pain and impending death held by people according to their religious and cultural beliefs or based on past experiences of friends and relatives who have died in pain.

It is important to ensure that relatives and friends are as fully involved as they wish to be (as long as the resident so wishes it). Staff should be alert to mood changes in the resident and his or her relatives and friends and offer support when required and provide necessary information (both about the condition of the resident and about practical matters). Information about the comforting benefits of some alternative therapies may also be useful in some circumstances.

## 5.8    Aids to care-giving

Managers and staff should be aware of the numerous ways by which the comfort of residents can be enhanced and the quality of care improved. Managers have a duty to ensure that information is kept up to date and shared with staff.  Specific advice and information should be obtained from appropriate professional staff or specialist organisations (*see Appendix 3 for further details*).

### 5.8.1  Mobility

There are a number of ways in which the mobility of residents can be improved, for example by ensuring that:

- walking aids are the correct height and length;
- wheelchairs are properly used and staff are trained how to transfer people in and out of them; electric wheelchairs are particularly useful in promoting residents' independence but take up more room and are more costly;
- supportive and properly fitting footwear, important in helping mobility, is available (slippers may impede mobility);
- the local community chiropody service, which should be involved in caring for residents' feet, is called in when necessary.

### 5.8.2  Continence

Appropriate advice and help with continence problems can improve the quality of life for an individual. It should not, however, be assumed that all individuals will be incontinent. There should be an active programme to promote continence which covers the full range of continence factors. One of the most telling indicators of poor care and practice is a stale urine smell. It should not be present in any home. In all cases of incontinence, improvements can be made or the impact reduced. Advice and information should be sought from a local continence nurse or advisor. The following factors are important:

- a positive management and staff attitude is required, supported by regular training. The distress caused to residents through incontinence should be recognised and sensitively and discreetly handled. Continence promotion programmes for the individual and for the home as a whole should be in place. Individual continence and toileting requirements should be recorded on care plans;

- a healthy diet should be followed with sufficient fluid (8-10 cups a day) and fibre to aid bowel movements;
- easy-to-use or adapted clothing may be helpful for some people;
- incidence of incontinence (urine or faeces) or changes in pattern should be investigated to see if there is any medical cause and appropriate treatment given. Particularly important are unwanted effects of drugs or urinary tract infection;
- for people with dementia it is important to establish a regular pattern in going to the toilet (as distinct from a 'toileting regime' which is organised for the benefit of staff and may make the problem for the resident worse);
- bladder training or strengthening pelvic floor muscles may be appropriate. Pelvic floor exercises could be included in any keep fit or exercise sessions. Reduced mobility may be a factor for some people so improving mobility may be beneficial;
- toilets should be well designed and easy to use. They should be kept clean. Any supplies of continence pads should be discreetly stored in closed cupboards and not left open to view;
- there should be an adequate number of toilets around the building close to living rooms, communal areas and bedrooms (where they are not en suite). They should be clearly identified, perhaps using a common coloured door throughout the building (and different from any other door);
- staffing levels should be such that help is immediately and reliably, yet unobtrusively, available for those who need it. Privacy should be maintained. Independence should be encouraged but people should not be left stranded sitting on the toilet. Toilet doors should not be left open, but should be able to be opened from outside when locked;
- the environment should not indicate that continence is expected – for example through the use of plastic-covered chairs, absence of carpets, overt bed protection, or exposed supplies of pads;
- wet and soiled clothes, furnishings and carpets should be cleaned immediately. Carpets, furniture and clothing in which smells develop should be thoroughly cleaned;
- commodes should only be used in a resident's room and if the resident so wishes. They should be emptied immediately after use

(at the latest first thing in the morning). Pans should be transported properly covered and be fully cleaned before being returned. Commodes should not be used in shared accommodation unless privacy can be assured;

- continence pads and other aids should only be used when absolutely necessary (and not to allow reduced staffing levels). The correct pad or appliance should be used. Pads should be changed immediately when wet or dirty;
- catheters should be inserted and used only under medical or nursing supervision. They should only be used when medically necessary and never to compensate for poor practice or inadequate resources. Staff should be fully trained in their use. Bags should be emptied and cleaned regularly and should not be left exposed;
- the active involvement of the local continence advisor, usually employed by the community health services trust or health authority, should be requested.

*The use of hoists*

Hoists may be necessary for lifting residents unable to move themselves from bed to chair, chair to toilet, chair to bath, but consideration should be given to minimising the stress which may result. Staff should ensure that the hoist is used correctly and that constant comfort and reassurance is given.

### 5.8.3 Hearing

It is likely that a substantial proportion of the residents of any home will have some hearing impairment. Although hearing loss is not an inevitable part of the ageing process, it does increase with age. Because it usually develops gradually, it tends to go unnoticed, resulting in the individual's sense of isolation. It may be a particular problem for people with dementia. It hampers the ability to join in general activities and to engage in conversation with other people, especially in rooms where there is a lot of background noise. The home should develop a coherent approach to handling the difficulties arising from hearing loss. It should involve the following:

- staff should be introduced to 'hearing awareness' as part of their induction and general training;

- managers, staff and volunteers should avoid shouting, should develop other ways of attracting attention (perhaps by writing), speak clearly, cut out background noise and check that they are being understood;
- examining ears for wax and removing it (by a GP or nurse) may be a straightforward way of improving an individual's hearing;
- the supply and maintenance of hearing aids, and training in their use, will bring about substantial improvement for many people. It may be appropriate to train one member of staff to be responsible for helping residents to use hearing aids. Batteries need to be checked regularly and frequently;
- other technical aids may be useful such as induction loops in communal rooms, visual door and telephone 'bells';
- residents should be encouraged to have hearing tests regularly and arrangements for tests to be conducted by the local audiology department should be established;
- eyesight tests are also important for people who rely on lipreading to communicate;
- specialist advice available from local social services/work departments (the designated social worker for deafness) or voluntary organisations should be sought on a regular basis.

### 5.8.4 Sight

Visual impairment can contribute to an individual's sense of isolation and separation from the life of the rest of the home. It may also limit mobility and jeopardise safety if measures are not taken to counter some of the difficulties. Among measures which can be taken are:
- the inclusion in the care plan of the last date of an eye test and the name of the optician. If this is not known, residents should be encouraged to have regular eye tests and arrangements should be made with local opticians/optometrists to provide them;
- the seeking of medical advice on cataracts and other eye conditions which may be amenable to clinical intervention. The links between poor vision and certain medical conditions (such as diabetes) should be recognised;
- the provision of simple technical aids, such as magnifying glasses and adequate lighting in the home, to assist getting around easily and for reading and other detailed activity;

- the use of large print in all public notices and in information and literature provided by the home for residents;
- access to large-print reading material and taped material;
- attention to signing in the home (door nameplates and staff badges, if worn) making sure they are big and clear enough to read at a distance;
- checking that residents' spectacles are clean should be part of the regular procedures of the day.

## 5.8.5 Dental care

Failure to ensure that residents' dental health is attended to can have repercussions in other aspects of their lives. Poor dental health can lower morale and make it difficult for people to eat nourishing food. It can also cause illness. Badly fitting dentures are particularly likely to cause problems and also to create social difficulties, for example at mealtimes in the company of other people.

Dental hygiene is important and residents should be encouraged to maintain their dental health on a daily basis and have dental checks undertaken by dentists and hygienists. If a resident does not have a regular dentist, arrangements should be made by the home with local dental practices to supply their services to the residents making it clear whether or not NHS treatment is available.

## 5.8.6 Diet

The food that is served to residents should be regarded as part of the general process of care-giving within the home. It should be palatable, nutritious and attractive to ensure that residents eat properly to maintain their health. Every effort should be made to determine and meet residents' food preferences. In particular, medical and cultural needs in relation to diet should be met. For everyone, a wholesome, adequate diet is as much a part of good care as is the provision of nursing and medical care.

# Management, administration and legal issues

## 6.1 Introduction

Sound management and administration provide the foundation for running a home well and for ensuring that the principles of high quality care and respect for residents can be put into practice.

## 6.2 Fitness

### 6.2.1 A fit person

Under the Registered Homes Act 1984 a person registered must be a fit and proper person to run a home. This means he or she should be trained and capable of managing a home and have the relevant business and professional experience. He or she must not have a criminal record nor have been barred from running a home by another registration authority. Since 1991, the registration authority can check whether new applicants for registration have criminal records; they can also request retrospective checks on existing registered persons if they can show sufficient cause for concern. In the case of nursing homes, the person in charge, although not necessarily the registered person, must be a level one qualified nurse or registered medical practitioner.

### 6.2.2 Fitness of premises

The premises must be judged suitable by the registration authority for use as a home in terms of their situation, construction, state of repair, accommodation, staffing and equipment.

### 6.2.3 Fitness of purpose

The registration authority must also be assured that the services and facilities offered meet the home's stated aims and objectives. These relate to choice, privacy, the opportunity for consultation, and general accommodation and services for residents.

## 6.3 The role of the manager

The tasks of a manager include the management of staff, the supervision of care (in the case of nursing homes), the efficient administration of the organisation (record-keeping, domestic organisation, legal matters, financial affairs, upkeep of the buildings and gardens), the management of supplies, support services such as laundry, cleaning, catering and gardening. Perhaps most importantly, the manager of the home is responsible for setting the tone and style of the home in terms of its efficiency, its probity, its concern for residents and staff, and its relationships with the outside world. A good leader can have a major impact on the way care is delivered and the standards which are achieved.

## 6.4 Record-keeping in relation to residents

### 6.4.1 Records

Certain records, detailed in the Residential Care Homes Regulations 1984 and the Nursing Home Regulations 1984, must be open to inspection by the registration authority on request. Personal details in these records should be kept in a secure place and access should be limited to those with overall responsibility for the day-to-day care of the resident. Anyone who has access to records should be instructed in the proper handling of confidential information. Managers and staff should be adequately briefed on issues relating to confidentiality and access to case files.

As well as those records required to be kept by law, such as personal details and next of kin, the home should keep other records:

- a care plan which is agreed with the resident and relevant care staff;
- a resident's life story book (particularly important for maintaining and restoring a person's sense of identity and as a source of information for staff);
- financial records, detailing payments made to the home;
- agreements entered into for accommodation;

- agreements for particular services and care not included in the overall agreement.

### 6.4.2 Residents' access to personal records

It is good practice for staff to share information with residents in the context of an open, professional relationship. Residents who wish to have access to their health records have a right in law to do so (Access to Health Records Act 1990). Under the Data Protection Act 1984, except in exceptional circumstances, people have the right of access to computerised records held on them. In some instances, counselling should be offered where sensitive information is disclosed. Some additional guidelines should be observed:
- information about a third party should not be disclosed without the consent of that party;
- information derived from a third party should not be disclosed without the consent of that party.

## 6.5 Management and administrative records

Homes should produce an 'aims and objectives' document underpinning the day-to-day work of the home which is regularly reviewed and updated. The home must display its certificate of registration, the only exception being homes catering for fewer than four residents. However, good practice suggests that displaying the certificate is a way of assuring prospective residents and their families and friends of the registered status of the home and even in the case of smaller homes it may be better to display the certificate. Records must be kept which set out details about the home and which must be available for inspection by the registration authorities. They should include:
- details of the home's registration;
- a list of all those in residence and their case records;
- a list of staff, their qualifications and their references;
- in the case of residential care homes, records of money or valuables kept on a resident's behalf;
- records relating to medication;
- records of complaints.

Under the regulations, residential care homes must keep records of residents for three years from the last entry. Nursing homes must retain case records for a year.

Other records which must be kept will relate to safety:

- maintenance records of specified equipment;
- records for health and safety purposes;
- records in line with fire regulations: precautions and practices undertaken and a list of those who will need help in the case of evacuation in a fire;
- records to meet food and hygiene regulations;
- records detailing accidents and other incidents.

Other documentation should include:

- the policies and procedures of the home;
- the residents' handbook (detailed information about life in the home and its fees and charges for various additional services);
- the staff handbook (which sets out terms and conditions of employment not included in individuals' statement of terms and conditions, general procedures at work and health and safety as it applies to staff members);
- staff rotas;
- staff records and employment procedures.

Financial systems should be in place which record:

- the collection of fees;
- salary and wages payments;
- tax payments.

## 6.6 Fees

### 6.6.1 Fee levels

Details should be set out clearly in agreements entered into at the time of moving into the home. They should specify in detail what is included in the fee and what services or elements of care are costed and charged for separately.

### 6.6.2 Increases in fees

Advance notice of any increase in fees and any consultation process should always be given. This is important both for individuals funding themselves and for residents who are funded by other sources. Local authorities will be closely involved in any changes in existing fee levels, particularly in relation to their contractual arrangements and service specifications with homes. Residents should not have to move because of changes in their funding arrangements if they are otherwise satisfied with the home. Neither should they have to move because of funding disputes between authorities or between an authority and the home.

## 6.7 Residents' money

Homeowners, managers and staff should never under any circumstances control residents' money. To do so may lay them open to suspicion of malpractice. Control of one's own finances is an important way of being able to be in control of one's life. In line with this, residents should handle their own money as far as they are able. If they can make their own arrangements for collecting their pensions they should be encouraged to do so. Where staff from the home act as agents and collect pensions in bulk, individual residents should receive their payments in private. When systems are in place in which staff have responsibility for the handling of residents' money, the registration authority should be informed of the arrangement and of the safeguards established to protect residents' interests (for example, residents should always sign that they have received the money). In some cases, homes may be able to operate a cheque-cashing service which may help residents who cannot get about easily.

Residents should be made aware that they are responsible for the safekeeping of their own money, documents such as pension books and other valuable possessions, unless they are unable to do so because of mental impairment. Residents should have a secure, lockable place within their own room for money and other personal valuables. Alternatively, if they wish, they should be able to place their valuables in a secure facility such as a safe or a lockable cupboard in, for example, the manager's office, with access strictly limited and controlled by the homeowner or manager. A clear record of this should be kept by the resident and the manager.

## 6.8 Group money and the home's amenity fund

Money collected for the benefit of the residents as a whole or for the home should not be used for routine expenditure. Residents should have a say in how it is spent. This means that there should be established ways of gathering residents' views in the home so that collective decisions can be made about how the money is used. The money which is collected should be lodged in a separate bank account with regular statements being made available to residents.

## 6.9 Legal issues

### 6.9.1 Appointments of agents, appointees, attorneys and trustees by residents

*Agents and appointees*
A resident may nominate a relative, friend or someone in the community over the age of eighteen to act as his or her agent in drawing and making payments. There is a well-established procedure for doing this for social security payments. If the resident wants a third party to operate his or her bank account then he or she can instruct a bank accordingly. When there is no relative or friend available whom the resident trusts, the Department of Social Security (DSS) should be asked to recommend someone to act as agent.

The homeowner, manager or staff members should not take on this role unless it has proved impossible to find an alternative. The DSS should be notified of residents for whom this arrangement is made. Such arrangements should be strictly limited to weekly payments and should not apply to any capital or assets.

In some circumstances, a relative, friend, or someone in the community such as an advocate, may become an appointee, able to make claims for and receive and deal with state benefits on behalf of the resident. In order to do so, an application needs to be made to the local DSS office. Social security regulations state that the claimant must be 'unable for the time being to act'. This usually means that the person does not have the mental capacity to look after his or her financial affairs, because of dementia, disease, or learning disability. Occasionally, the problem might be temporary, for example because of a serious accident.

The person to be appointed must demonstrate to the DSS that he or she would make the most suitable appointee and show an active interest in the welfare of the individual. Where an owner or manager is made an appointee the registration authority must be notified and individual records must be kept for inspection of monies coming in and going out. Once accepted, an appointee has a duty to ensure that the resident will get the full benefit of the payment made and that any changes in the circumstances of the resident which may affect his or her benefits are promptly reported.

Appointment under the social security regulations comes to an end: if it is revoked by the DSS; if the appointee resigns after giving one month's notice; or if the DSS is told that a receiver has been appointed by the Court of Protection for England and Wales, or a curator bonis (or other judicial factor) has been appointed by the Sheriff Court or Court of Session in Scotland, or in Northern Ireland the High Court appoints a controller of the person. The DSS must also be notified if either the claimant or the appointee dies.

*Power of attorney*
A power of attorney is an arrangement by which one individual (the donor) gives authority to another or others to act on his or her behalf. The attorney is required to act as if he or she were the donor. Appointing an attorney might be a good idea if a resident has difficulty getting out to the bank or building society, or has difficulty signing cheques or documents. However, power of attorney (like agency) cannot be used where the person does not have the mental capacity to give authorisation to the attorney.

The power can be used in specific or general areas of managing income and capital. Copies can be shown to banks, building societies, pension funds or insurance and pensions companies when required. At any time the donor can cancel the power of attorney. The attorney must demonstrate that he or she is taking proper care of the donor's affairs and may be sued for any loss due to insufficient care.

It is very important to realise that in England, Wales and Northern Ireland a power of attorney is automatically cancelled by operation of law when the individual loses mental capacity to manage his or her own affairs. An attorney who then continues to act is doing so without authority and is liable to be sued. Instead, the attorney should stop acting. The person's affairs may then have to be handled by the Court of Protection in England and Wales or the High Court and the Office of Care and Protection in Northern Ireland.

In Scotland it is possible to have a continuing power of attorney which is still valid even if the person loses capacity. The original document should state whether or not it continues after loss of capacity, but there does not have to be a special form like the enduring power of attorney (*see below*) and the deed does not have to be specially registered.

### Enduring power of attorney

Unlike an ordinary power of attorney, in England, Wales and Northern Ireland an enduring power of attorney (EPA) can continue in force even if the individual loses mental capacity. EPAs are often made by older people who are aware of failing mental faculties, but still have capacity to understand what is involved in creating an EPA. The EPA can give the attorney general power to act in relation to the donor's property and affairs, or can relate to specific items. An EPA must be made in a prescribed form laid down by law, and the person may wish to consult a solicitor or legal advisor and may appoint a solicitor or social services department to act as an attorney under an EPA. More often, the attorney chosen will be a son or daughter, spouse or other close relative.

An attorney under an EPA must take proper care of the donor's affairs and also takes on certain special duties. As soon as the attorney believes that the donor is or is becoming mentally incapable then the attorney must stop acting until the EPA has been registered by the Court of Protection in England and Wales or by the High Court in Northern Ireland. Again, this must be done in the correct prescribed form, with certain relatives of the donor (laid down by law) being informed. Once the EPA is registered, the attorney can safely start acting again. An EPA may, alternatively, stipulate that it should take effect only if mental incapacity should occur, in which case it would first need to be registered as above.

### Court of Protection

In England and Wales the Court of Protection exists to protect the interests of people who are unable to manage their own financial affairs because of mental disorder. The term 'mental disorder' is a legal label which includes dementia, learning disabilities and mental health problems.

The Court usually delegates power over the income of the person to a 'receiver' who can handle day-to-day matters. Capital is usually retained on deposit by the Court. Anyone can apply to be a receiver, giving full details of their finances and family situation (and paying a Court fee). Often a relative or solicitor applies, but it would be appropriate for someone such as an advocate to do so.

The responsibilities of the receiver are detailed in a handbook issued by the Court. The receiver is required to handle all financial transactions for the benefit of the person. All dealings are monitored by the Court which requires the submission of annual accounts. An annual fee is usually payable to the Court.

In Northern Ireland, the interests of people who are unable to manage their own financial affairs because of mental disorder are looked after by the High Court and the Office of Care and Protection. The High Court may delegate power over the income of the person to a 'controller' whose powers are the same as those of a receiver.

### Curator Bonis (Scotland only)

If a resident is unable to manage his or her financial affairs due to mental disorder, a curator bonis can be appointed. The appointment is made by the Sheriff Court on the basis of two medical reports. The curator takes over full responsibility for handling the person's finances and is required to follow detailed rules and act under the supervision of the Accountant of the Court.

### Trusts

Alternatively a resident may decide to set up a trust to manage his or her affairs. This is normally worth doing only if there are substantial assets but it has the great advantage of continuing to be valid even if the resident should cease to be mentally competent.

### Tutor dative (Scotland only)

A tutor dative is a kind of personal guardian. The tutor can exercise a range of powers on behalf of a person who is unable to act because of mental disorder. The powers can include deciding where a person should live, consenting on his or her behalf to medical treatment, deciding who should have access to a person, and initiating medical treatment.

Tutors are usually relatives, but others can be appointed. Strictly, they are decision-makers, not advocates. However, many tutors see the value of the appointment as giving them a 'voice' and status with service providers.

*Guardianship*
Under the Mental Health Act 1983 in England and Wales and the Mental Health (Scotland) Act 1984, a person who has one of four specified forms of 'mental disorder' may be received into guardianship if it is necessary for his or her own welfare or the protection of others. The guardian will almost always be the local social services/work authority as this form of 'guardianship' is a way of seeking compulsory control over a person who needs help. The guardian has the power to require the individual to live at a particular place, to attend particular places for medical treatment, occupation or training, and to require access to be given to doctors, social workers and others at any place where he or she resides. Application for guardianship is made to the local authority and must be supported by two doctors and an approved social worker or in Scotland a mental health officer.

Under the Mental Health (Northern Ireland) Order 1987, a person who has one of two specified forms of mental disorder may be received into guardianship if it is necessary for his or her own welfare. The guardian is generally the local health and social services board. The guardian has the same powers as in England and Wales. Application for guardianship is made to the local health and social services board, usually by an approved social worker, and must be accompanied by two medical recommendations and a recommendation by an approved social worker who is not the person making the application.

6.9.2  **Homeowners' and managers' responsibilities**
Homeowners have no legal obligation to defend the interests of residents who are no longer capable of looking after their financial affairs. However, they do have a duty to safeguard and promote the welfare of residents and it is recommended that they should initiate appropriate action when there is nobody else capable or willing to do so. Prior discussion with the registration authority is essential. If referral to the Court of Protection, the Court of Session or the High Court seems indicated, the appropriate action would be for the homeowner to draw the matter to the attention of the resident's GP and if he or she indicates a willingness to provide the

necessary medical recommendation then, in the absence of any appropriate person, the homeowner should contact the Court for advice and if necessary make the application himself or herself. Under no circumstances should anybody connected with the running of the home be appointed receiver.

As noted, those involved in the running of residential and nursing homes have no obligation to see that the law is complied with where residents' financial affairs are concerned, save where they become involved themselves in some way. However, if they feel that something (not necessarily of a legal nature) is going wrong, and the resident is unable to deal with it, homeowners should draw their fears to the attention of relatives or the registration authority, whichever is more appropriate.

This duty in no way contradicts the essential principle that all those connected with the running of a home should not become involved in the handling and management of a resident's financial affairs. Homeowners and managers are potentially vulnerable to accusations of misconduct. Suggestions of impropriety may be hard to dispel even if they are without foundation.

## 6.10 Advance statements about health care (living wills)

A resident with a progressive illness which could lead to loss of decision-making capacity in the future may wish to record his or her views about health care options. This might cover issues concerning refusal of treatment, requests for treatment and purposes of treatment. If the person then loses capacity and cannot participate in health care decisions, those involved in treatment and care would be able to take the previously expressed views into account. If the views are written down then the document is often called an 'advance directive' or 'living will'.

There is no legislation about living wills in the United Kingdom. There is some relevant English case law regarding advance directives to refuse particular treatment. However, there are many complex considerations and interests involved and the position is not clear in every possible situation.

## 6.11 Improving quality: procedures for making suggestions

Homeowners and managers should welcome suggestions for improving or adding to the life of the home. An open and friendly style of management will encourage this and prevent residents and their families and friends from feeling inhibited about raising issues, making comments or putting forward suggestions. Clear information about how to make suggestions should be provided. This might be through the provision of a suggestions book or a suggestions box. Staff should be ready to listen to ideas that residents express and pass them on to the manager.

## 6.12 Complaints procedures

There must (residential care homes) and should (nursing homes) be a clearly established complaints procedure which is described in information about the home and about which residents, their relatives and friends are told when the resident first moves in. Managers and staff should not assume that an absence of complaints means that everything is running smoothly. They should be particularly alert to the general hesitancy of residents and relatives to complain for fear (however unjustified) of recrimination. Residents and relatives may even be reluctant to make suggestions because they fear this may be seen as implied criticism. Residents may feel fearful and vulnerable and therefore unwilling to speak out because they are dependent on staff and managers for their care and assistance. More generally, it should be remembered that many older people tend to 'go along with things' in response to questions and that a comment to the effect that something is satisfactory could in fact indicate that improvements could be made. Advocates have a useful role in supporting residents in making a complaint and homeowners should welcome their involvement in the life of the home.

The information given to residents and relatives should stress that ideas, suggestions and complaints are welcome and expected. A complaints procedure should have the following features:
- it should set out clearly to whom the complaint in the first instance should be made and indicate to whom the resident can complain if he or she remains dissatisfied;

- it should make an explicit commitment which states that matters will be taken seriously and prompt action will result if the complaint is justified;
- it should contain assurances that residents will not be victimised as a result of making a complaint;
- it should assure fairness and impartiality and offer access to an impartial third party if the resident so wishes;
- it should provide clear and concise written responses if the resident wishes;
- it should guarantee that action will be taken to ensure no repetition if the complaint is shown to be valid;
- it should offer an apology if the complaint is valid;
- it should offer compensation if appropriate;
- it should make clear the further procedure which includes complaining to the registration authority which can require information about complaints and their resolution if they fall within the provision of the Registered Homes Act 1984.

Any infringement of this code of practice should be considered a legitimate cause for complaint.

# Staffing

## 7.1 Introduction

The quality of life which residents experience will depend to a great extent on the calibre of the staff caring for them. A trained and experienced staff team, which is well managed and adequately paid, is likely to provide high quality care in a responsive and understanding atmosphere. People living in residential and nursing homes are often vulnerable, both physically and emotionally. Staff will be required to carry out personal and potentially embarrassing intimate services for residents and will need special qualities to do this sensitively and tactfully. Such qualities will include personal warmth, patience and responsiveness to and respect for the individual. They should be able to provide competent and tactful care whilst supporting residents in maintaining and extending skills and self-care abilities.

## 7.2 The staff team

If residents are to receive a satisfactory standard of care, it is important that the staff see themselves as part of a team which is consistent in its shared aims, with members fulfilling complementary roles. A balance of staff will therefore need to be appointed to match the residents' needs.

There are four main groups of staff in the home to consider in developing the staff team:

- managerial staff (which includes the homeowner or manager in overall charge, and in larger homes other managers or supervisors of staff);
- day care staff and night care staff (which includes nurses and care assistants as appropriate);

- administrative and clerical staff (such as finance officer, secretary and records staff);
- ancillary staff (which includes cleaners, laundry staff, catering staff, building maintenance staff, gardeners).

In addition, the role to be played by peripatetic staff such as occupational therapists and chiropodists and by volunteers will need to be considered carefully.

Current law requires that homes be run with an adequate number of staff who have the right balance of skills and experience to meet the needs of residents. Before registration, therefore, a prospective owner must draw up a staffing schedule to show how the staff team meets the residents' requirements. The schedule is subject to inspection and approval by the inspection and registration authority and the onus is on the applicant for registration to provide sufficient evidence that the right level of staffing with appropriate competence and training will be provided. Different sized homes and levels of residents' dependency will require different staffing complements. Nursing homes must have a registered medical practitioner or first level registered nurse as the person in charge as well as employing other qualified nursing staff for nursing duties. The registration authority ultimately determines the staffing levels and skill mix appropriate to the needs and dependency of residents in each nursing home and sets it out in a staffing notice before registration.

It is not acceptable for a home to be left in the control of a person with insufficient training and experience. The staffing establishment and rota system therefore need to be arranged so that there are enough senior staff and they are suitably deployed to give the cover required to meet the home's stated aims.

## 7.3 Staff recruitment and selection

### 7.3.1 Recruitment

The recruitment of good staff is critical to the running of every home and should be undertaken carefully. Staff at all levels will need to demonstrate the right degree of knowledge, skills, experience and attitudes relevant to their jobs. Managerial and supervisory staff will need to have qualifications as appropriate.

The following stages are involved:
- advertisements should be clear about the sort of person wanted and the work they will do;
- comprehensive information should be available for potential applicants;
- a person specification and job description should be drawn up;
- application forms should be completed by all people applying for jobs (with the amount of detail appropriate for the job);
- the interviewing process should be conducted fairly by senior staff with the appropriate skills. It should include candidates talking to residents and existing staff;
- references should be taken up from two people, one at least from a previous employer or from someone who, for example, has supervised the applicant in a volunteer capacity (rather than a character reference from a friend);
- references should be written and sent directly by the referee, and where necessary followed up with a telephone call to check statements;
- employment histories should be checked for any gaps or evidence of misconduct;
- prospective employees must disclose all previous criminal convictions including those which are 'otherwise spent'. The Rehabilitation and Offenders Act 1974 (Exemptions) Order 1975 requires residential and nursing home care staff to disclose previous convictions. Since 1991, police checks for owners and managers of homes can be made through the registration authority;
- the authenticity of qualifications should be checked;
- a health declaration should be requested before appointment;
- proper records of the recruitment process should be kept.

The same criteria should be applied in deciding whether to appoint relatives of homeowners' families to work in the home.

*Equal opportunities*
It is sometimes difficult to balance equal opportunities procedures with the needs and rights of residents. The recruitment procedures and the composition of the staff team should as far as possible match the mix of cultural and language backgrounds of residents.

*Resident involvement*

Consideration should be given to possible ways of involving residents in the selection of staff. For example, where a new member of staff will be working with a small group of residents, the final choice could be made by the resident group after management has screened for suitability. Where residents are involved they may need help to take part in a selection process.

Advice on good practice in employment procedures can be sought from registration and inspection authorities, employment agencies, and independent bodies such as the Advisory, Conciliation and Arbitration Service (ACAS).

## 7.3.2 Job descriptions

Job descriptions should describe the roles and tasks which staff have to undertake. They should outline the management structure and lines of accountability and the support and supervision available. They should also set out the overall purpose of the job, linking the importance of the tasks described to the aims of the home as a whole.

## 7.3.3 Terms and conditions of employment

Recent employment law has made it mandatory for certain terms and conditions of employment to be clearly stated in writing and given to each employee as part of the contract of employment. It is good practice to cover:

- remuneration;
- hours of duty;
- length of probationary period;
- grievance and disciplinary procedures;
- period of notice or dismissal;
- trades union recognition (or not);
- holiday entitlement;
- sickness payments;
- pension arrangements;
- maternity and paternity benefits;
- redundancy;
- commitment to an equal opportunities policy;
- training opportunities.

It needs to be recognised that a high turnover of staff in a home is often an indicator of low quality. Where terms and conditions of employment are poor – with low pay, low status, inadequate training opportunities and lack of career development – staff are unlikely to remain on a long-term basis. This in turn will have an impact on the quality of care provided within the home.

## 7.3.4 Staff handbook

A detailed handbook should be readily available for each member of staff, setting out terms and conditions of employment as above and also covering procedures to be observed during working hours. It may be an integral part of, or an appendix to, the contract of employment. It should include:

- terms and conditions of employment;
- health and safety at work policies;
- procedures in specific circumstances, for example fire and other emergencies;
- policies and procedures relating to sickness and absences;
- instructions on maintaining confidentiality;
- instructions on receiving gifts or gratuities and not being involved in the drawing up of wills.

## 7.3.5 Induction

New members of staff should be given a job induction during which they are introduced to residents and other members of staff and the nature of their job described. The aims and objectives of the home and its routines and procedures (especially fire and safety) should be set out for them, along with the standards of care which all members of staff are expected to achieve.

## 7.3.6 Probationary period

It is good employment practice for all staff to undergo a formal probationary period to ensure that they are suitable for the job and the home. They should be properly supported during this time with a review undertaken at the end of the period. Care should be taken to ensure that new staff are not placed on duty together and unsupported. It is good practice to place a new member of staff alongside a more experienced person who can act as mentor.

## 7.4    Working conditions

### 7.4.1    Hours of duty

Duty rotas should be based on a working week of 36 to 40 hours. Staff should not be expected to work additional hours regularly or to work more than seven days continuously without taking a break. Rotas should therefore pay attention to both shift patterns and time off duty. Care should be taken to ensure that enough time and attention is given to handover procedures between shifts so that staff coming on duty are fully informed about any developments or changes in residents' circumstances.

### 7.4.2    Dress

Clothing worn by staff should be suitable for the tasks that they have to carry out. There are arguments for and against uniforms. They tend to give an institutional feel to an establishment but if a majority of residents express a preference for staff to wear them then it may be appropriate. It is most important, however, that uniforms do not create a misleading impression that staff are nurses (if they are not) or that staff are qualified (if they are not). Staff from ethnic minorities should be able to wear their own style of dress.

Other options include a corporate colour, style or item of clothing. Name badges can be helpful, particularly where there is a large staff team or if residents find it difficult to remember names. They are also helpful for visitors. They may be more suitable if they are sewn names on cloth badges (rather than hard badges or brooches where there is a risk of scratching residents) and large enough to be read by residents with poor sight. Jewellery such as brooches, chains and rings should either be covered or not worn if it might scratch or harm residents.

Attention should always be given to matters of infection control, either from resident to resident, resident to staff or staff to resident, and so practical protective clothing should be available for staff when needed.

### 7.4.3    Support for staff

Managers should ensure that managerial structures, communications systems and staff supervision are sufficient to enable staff to undertake their duties effectively.

Staff induction, manuals of guidance, in-house training, staff meetings and individual supervision should be considered carefully and laid out in detail. The extent to which staff need these forms of support will depend on the complexity and stress involved in their work. It is important to remember that in the event of a crisis or an enquiry, homeowners may have to demonstrate that the support structures which they had in place were sufficient. Good working relationships will be enhanced if all levels of staff are included in discussions about the running of the home.

*Staff meetings*
Staff meetings should take place regularly and involve all staff. They should normally be held in paid time and be arranged if necessary on a rotating basis, so that all staff, including night staff, can participate over a period of time.

*Staff supervision*
There should be one-to-one supervision sessions for all staff on a regular basis although they may be required more frequently for nursing and care staff than other staff categories. The sessions should enable managers to ensure that staff are performing satisfactorily and provide opportunities for constructive criticism and understanding support. Personal and career development should be discussed. In larger homes, delegated supervision may need to be arranged.

*Stress*
Working in the care environment can be stressful. Staff have to learn to cope with death, serious illness and the difficult behaviour of some residents. For a home to be able to deal with such things as high levels of incontinence and aggressive and violent behaviour, managers should have policies and procedures in place which ensure enough support and training opportunities for staff and adequate staffing levels.

## 7.5   Staffing establishments

Homeowners need to demonstrate that they have considered the residents' needs in relation to all types of staff in drawing up their staffing establishments. They will therefore need to set out the numbers of staff, their designations and duties, their gradings or salaries attached to posts, and the types of qualifications, experience and training which will be expected for each post. It is important to indicate the balance between part-time and full-time posts since part-time work allows for more flexible deployment while full-time posts tend to improve consistency and continuity of care. In larger homes there may be scope for some posts to be specialist but in smaller homes staff may carry a wider variety of responsibilities, including managerial work, resident care, cooking and so on. In all cases, however, the duties required of staff should be made clear at the time of appointment and any changes of duty or role should be recorded in writing.

### 7.5.1  Residential care homes: managerial and care staff

*Minimum cover*

In drawing up their management and care staffing establishments, owners should consider two main factors. The first is the provision of minimum cover. There must be a 'responsible person' designated on duty at all times during the twenty-four hour day. This means that there is someone present who can make decisions in an emergency, who is familiar with the home's procedures and practices and has the necessary skills and training to manage the service provided. In larger homes or those where the work is more demanding, either physically or in terms of residents' behaviour, minimum staffing levels will be higher, and generally two staff will be needed at any one time where residents have to be lifted.

As a rule of thumb, with allowance made for time off, holidays and some illness, a home needs to employ 3.5 staff to provide one person on day duty. Where at least two staff are needed on duty at all times, the minimum cover would therefore demand 3.5 x 2 = 7.00 staff. These figures are given in full-time equivalents, but could be filled by part-time staff where appropriate, or a mixture of full- and part-timers.

These approximate minimum staffing figures are based upon a full-time working week of 36 to 40 hours. Where owners, managers or other senior staff are resident and are prepared to be available on call for longer periods, minimum staffing calculations may take this into account. Adequate cover will need to be assured, however, when some resident staff are absent; remaining resident staff should not have excessive demands placed upon them. Owners' or managers' dependent relatives living on the premises may also be taken into account when cover is assessed. Where married couples are the owners or are employed, care should be taken to ensure that they have reasonable time off together each week and for holidays, and that they are not under pressure to forego this right for lack of staffing.

The minimum cover set out here is designed to cope with the general running of the home but there are peaks and troughs in the residents' demand for staff support and help. Peaks include getting up, mealtimes, activities and going to bed; troughs include times when residents are out of the building and rest periods. It is important, therefore, not only to provide minimum cover but also to deploy staff to offer additional support at peak periods. The employment of part-time staff can enable such deployment to be flexible without causing problems such as split shifts for full-timers.

*Total staff required*

The second main factor in the calculation of day care staffing is the degree of need presented by the residents and the consequent amount of staff time required. Needs will vary, particularly between homes which are registered as residential care homes and those which are registered as nursing homes, but even amongst residential homes themselves needs will vary. Total requirements can be arrived at by estimating the number of care hours required according to residents' needs per week and then totalled per resident per annum, and then totalled for the home as a whole. Thus the number of staff needed can be worked out once allowance is made for holidays, illness and other absences. This approach gives the total staffing required for all managerial and care staff on day duties, inclusive of the minimum cover outlined above. Even where an establishment is geared towards encouraging self-care and participation in household tasks, there can generally be no staffing reduction as staff will still be needed to help in these activities – although residents who become increasingly independent will sometimes need less support.

Allowance has also to be made for leave, sickness, training, staff meetings and other activities. Where senior staff are involved in client selection, recruitment of staff, fundraising and additional extraneous duties, further allowance will need to be made. In general, a full-time employee can provide about 1,500 hours of care time per annum.

There are a number of different models available which cover this issue. One such model is contained in a handbook produced by the Wagner Development Group. It gives guidance on calculating staffing establishments and is helpful to owners and managers in establishing a staff team (*see Appendix 2*).

*Night staffing*

Night staffing requirements will depend upon the mobility and lucidity of residents on the one hand, and the type of handling problems anticipated on the other. Where residents require lifting, for example, two members of staff are needed, regardless of the size of the home. In order to calculate the staffing required, an establishment of 2.5 full-time equivalents is sufficient to provide one person on duty although this does not take into account periods of cover for sickness, annual leave or training. Where waking staff on duty are not sufficiently experienced and trained, it will be necessary for senior staff to sleep 'on call' on the premises.

7.5.2 **Nursing homes: managerial and nursing staff**

The person in charge of a nursing home must be a registered medical practitioner or a first level registered nurse. The registration authority specifies by notice the qualifications of staff and minimum staffing levels required in a nursing home, and when drawing up the notice it will need to be satisfied as to the arrangements for the management and control of the services to be provided. This will include the arrangements for the delegation of responsibilities and supervision of staff. At least one first level nurse should be on duty throughout the day. The registration authority may decide that a second level registered nurse may be in charge during the night, but that nurse must be fully appraised of the general nursing needs of all residents. A first level nurse should be nominated to be 'on call' where a second level nurse is in charge at night. The current registration of all qualified nursing staff should be checked with the United Kingdom Central Council for Nursing, Midwifery and Health-visiting (UKCC).

*Nursing levels*

It is not possible to specify standard staffing ratios because of the variation in needs and circumstances of residents in different nursing homes. The NAHAT handbook (*see Appendix 2*) outlines the variety of factors which need to be taken into account in determining staff mix and staff levels. These include:

- the number and type of residents;
- whether a medical practitioner lives on the premises and, if not, his or her distance away from the home;

- the size and design of the building (including the number of floors);
- the means of evacuation of residents in the case of fire, especially at night;
- the dependency levels of residents and their need for nursing, especially at night;
- the range of additional non-nursing duties expected of nursing auxilliaries in addition to direct care of residents.

On the basis of these factors and others as described in the NAHAT handbook, the registration authority will determine the number and type of qualified nursing staff to be employed and the ratio of trained to untrained staff. The same range of factors as in 7.5.1 above will need to be taken into account in determining levels of non-nursing staff.

7.5.3 **Ancillary staff**

Ancillary staffing includes staff not primarily engaged to undertake managerial, nursing or social care roles, but the value of their contact with residents or their therapeutic role should not be underestimated. In large establishments the management of ancillary staff is likely to require experience and a different set of skills. While no specific guidelines are offered for the numbers of such staff, owners should consider the tasks listed below.

*Cooking*

In some homes, care staff may do the cooking to help create a homely atmosphere, or, in larger establishments, it may be done by full-time cooks. The approach should be determined by the overall aim of the home, and appropriate training made available to ensure that residents obtain a varied, balanced diet that also reflects their individual wishes.

*Laundry work and needlework*

In large homes, or where incontinence presents major problems, consideration may be given to the appointment of staff to deal solely with laundry. Needlework may be undertaken by residents or care staff, but there may be homes where a needleworker should be appointed to care for residents' clothes. It is important in both laundering and needlework that residents' clothing is well looked after, since carelessness may not only damage the clothes but seriously upset residents and their families who see it as a sign of institutional treatment.

*Domestic work*

Communal areas will normally be cleaned by paid staff, even in homes where residents are encouraged to clean their private rooms. Old buildings are sometimes more difficult to clean and will require extra time and attention.

*Gardening and maintenance*

This work may be carried out by owners, care staff, residents or outside contractors. In some circumstances, however, staff may be appointed to carry out maintenance work, since good maintenance is important for the comfort of residents, especially when they are dependent on the efficient functioning of heating systems, hot water supplies, other household systems and aids with which the home is equipped.

*Clerical work and administration*

It is important that both the care and managerial aspects of the home are properly backed by clerical and administrative staff, to ensure that residents' records, correspondence, appointments, financial records and general administration are kept up to date, without using senior managerial time inappropriately.

## 7.6   Training and staff development

Managers should enable and encourage staff to undertake training. There are now a number of schemes throughout the country which residential and nursing home staff can join which provide skills training of various sorts. As part of staff appraisal and supervision, an individual training and development plan should be drawn up for all staff (new and existing). Staff should be encouraged to undertake training courses to acquire skills and, where appropriate, qualifications. The benefits to be derived from having a trained staff are many:

- residents receive better care;
- staff feel more confident that they are doing the work as it should be done and that they can tackle problems that arise;
- staff feel valued by management when the training programme has the management's backing;
- the ethos of the home is improved;
- a pool of staff is available for promotion and career progression.

It is sometimes easier to provide training in-house than to arrange for staff to spend time away. In-house training of this kind should be seen as an integral part of the running of the establishment and emphasis should be given to the timing and arrangement of staffing rotas to ensure relief cover is provided to enable staff to receive training. Night staff should be included in all training opportunities. Training costs money and this will have to be incorporated into the fees charged to residents and their funders. There are a range of courses and types of training available from which to choose:

- in-house training provided by colleagues who themselves are skilled;
- peer group training;
- distance learning (for example via the Open University, the Royal Institute of Public Health and Hygiene);
- courses provided by local Training and Enterprise Councils (TECs) and colleges, university departments, hospital teaching departments;
- courses organised by care homes associations;
- clinical placements.

The most common formal training qualifications that staff in homes work for are National Vocational Qualifications (NVQs) and Scottish Vocational Qualifications (SVQs). Five levels of qualifications are set out within the NVQ and SVQ framework. At level 2 (which is the level most often worked towards by care staff), competence is expected in a variety of work activities, some complex and non-routine, along with the ability to work both alone and in collaboration with others in different situations.

At level 2, there are currently nine NVQs/SVQs in care available:

- developmental care;
- domiciliary support;
- post-natal care;
- combined support;
- activity and access support;
- direct care;
- residential/hospital support;
- special care needs;
- independent living support.

Care staff in residential and nursing homes find the combined support and direct care awards particularly relevant.

The NVQ/SVQ system of training covers staff at all levels, including managerial training, and many providers are now linking career and pay progression to the achievement of specific NVQ/SVQ levels. For example, a care manager may require a level 3 in care and a level 4 in management, a home manager a level 3 in care and a level 5 in management (as equivalent to professional qualifications such as CSS or CQSW).

The importance of training for all staff, particularly those who have direct contact with residents, cannot be over-emphasised. In particular, staff (both care staff and ancillary staff) will benefit from training in guarding against abuse, promoting continence, and caring for those who are dying. In the case of residents who have dementia, it is important that those who have most contact with them understand their symptoms and know how best to handle those symptoms. This will have a bearing on many aspects of residents' daily lives – getting dressed, activities, meal-times, going out, going to bed. It is also important for staff to receive training on health and safety issues, particularly, for example, in relation to food safety, manual handling and the use of hoists.

# Buildings

## 8.1 Principles

The design of the home is an important influence on the residents' quality of life. Design should be geared to satisfying the needs of residents and staff providing care within the home. A well-designed home will:

- provide a safe and secure environment for residents;
- ensure their privacy and provide their own personal space under their own control;
- protect their dignity;
- offer them a stimulating setting for daily activities;
- enable them to have easy access around the home;
- minimise residents' difficulties in understanding their surroundings;
- provide a work setting which enables staff to deliver high quality care;
- meet the standards relating to the design and fabric of residential and nursing homes required by law, regulations and directives.

Over time, expectations have risen and standards are continually improving. Prospective residents will look for homes where they can expect many of the features outlined here.

## 8.2 Location and setting

If a home is to be newly built, then careful consideration should be given to its location and setting as part of the preparatory process. These, along with its accessibility to public transport, local shops and other community facilities such as pubs and libraries, are likely to influence the choice of individuals and their families.

### 8.2.1 Access to the local community

It is important that a home should not feel isolated from the surrounding community. In some cases residents may be frail and unable to get out and about but they are still likely to value links with the local community, schools, community organisations and places of worship.

### 8.2.2 Transport

If residents cannot get about by themselves, the home should consider hiring or purchasing its own transport for outings and trips to shops and places of worship, or arrange for friends, relatives and volunteers to provide it. Such help might also be arranged for relatives and friends who have no transport of their own and who cannot use public transport. Car parking for visitors (and residents in some cases) should be available.

### 8.2.3 Views and aspect

First impressions of a home – its setting and the building itself – will have an important impact on potential residents. Open views on to gardens or on to scenes of activity (such as a school or a street) may be important for different individuals. Good landscape design and planting at the initial development stage of a new home will be a worthwhile investment in terms both of resident satisfaction and in enhancing the value of the property.

Homes should make clear in their brochures the advantages of their location and accessibility.

## 8.3 Building design

This code recognises that most homes have not been purpose-built and that many have been open for a period of years. Building work is expensive and in any case many existing buildings may not be amenable to adaptation and improvement. The cost implications of some improvements (for example, conversion of rooms into single rooms with en suite facilities) will have revenue as well as capital consequences.

At present, properties do not have to be brought in line with current local authority building regulations on change of ownership; however, under the Registered Homes Act 1984, it is possible to impose new requirements on the new owner. Although this may seem unfair, clearly homeowners should be aware of this possibility. Many of the standards outlined here can be described as 'best practice' which all homes should seek to achieve over time. All homes should have a policy of continuous improvement and this should take account of the standards outlined in this document. A plan and timetable for attainment of the standards laid down in the policy should be drawn up and progress against it monitored regularly.

This should not be taken as a reason to avoid meeting certain standards below which quality should not be allowed to fall under any circumstances. These are the standards which guarantee the privacy and dignity of residents, promote their independence and enable them to live their lives in the way that suits them best. Some are contained in legislation, regulations and guidance; others will be set by national associations (of the professions, homeowners and others) or be the outcome of agreement between homeowners and inspection and registration units. The standards outlined in this code can provide a basis for such agreements.

### 8.3.1 Purpose-built

In line with the trend which has developed in recent years, the population of residential and nursing homes is likely to become frailer and more dependent in the future. New purpose-built homes should take this into account from the outset. All new homes should be built with single occupancy accommodation with en suite toilet and washing facilities (this should not preclude the possibility of couples, friends, relatives from sharing accommodation if so wished, through, for example, being able to use two rooms, one as bedroom and one as living room). The standards and guidance outlined here should be incorporated into all newly built homes, particularly in relation to issues of privacy, control, activity, adaptations, room size, and features which minimise confusion. This applies equally to newly built extensions to existing properties.

### 8.3.2 Improvements

Where homes are already established, opportunities should be taken to improve the accommodation as and when possible, either as part of the development programme or, for example, when redecorations are being carried out or between residencies.

Such improvements may include:

- phasing out all shared rooms (apart from one or two for couples);
- using former double rooms for small lounges or dining rooms, for single rooms with en suite facilities or for activity rooms;
- where practicable, adding en suite facilities to rooms;
- adopting a policy of redecoration between residencies, ideally with the new resident taking responsibility for deciding what should be done;
- personalising doors with nameplates or pictures;
- changing the use of communal areas for community activities or day care for older people from outside the home (especially if smaller lounges and dining rooms have been created);
- building a sun lounge;
- improving access to the garden and incorporating new features – for example, sheltered areas, raised flowerbeds.

### 8.3.3 Architects and other professional advisors

When designing a new building or an extension, it is important to use an architect and builder who understand the needs of older people and the principles of good practice. Their previous work should be reviewed and if possible visited. Homes inspectors should be consulted, along with other professional staff, for example occupational therapists, landscape gardeners, crime prevention officers, security consultants.

## 8.4 Size of home and living units

The size of home will be determined by many factors: the size of an existing building, the style and purpose of the organisation, the relative costs involved. Whatever the size, though, the principles of good quality care outlined in this code should be observed. How they are put into practice will relate to the scale of the operation and will involve:

- the capacity of the residents and the level of care given;
- the daily pattern of life;
- the ethos of the home and its management philosophy;
- the attitudes and training of staff;
- the deployment of staff and duty rotas;
- the use of equipment and technology;
- the use of space within the home.

So long as the central aim is to support and enhance the quality of life for residents, the fostering of individuality and the maintenance of privacy and dignity, a variety of living arrangements is possible. Adherence to that central aim may compensate for shortfalls in the building itself.

## 8.4.1 Unit or group living

The aim should be, regardless of the overall size of the home, for life to be on a domestic scale for every resident. This can be achieved, particularly in larger settings, by breaking living arrangements into smaller units. In this way residents should be able to identify with a group of other residents however large or small the whole home may be. Each group or unit of this sort should be able to have its own small lounge or dining room with some facilities being shared with the other units, such as a kitchen, transport, communal lounge, garden, laundry or activity rooms. A group can then be cared for by a particular team of staff, thus facilitating the development of a sense of common identity.

## 8.4.2 People with dementia

There are particular advantages in looking after people with dementia in small groups and there are some proven therapeutic benefits in doing so. These may either be provided through a small home, or through group living as described above. There is some evidence to suggest that a group no larger than eight to twelve residents can best provide the individual care which people with dementia require.

## 8.4.3 Domestic style

Every effort should be made to prevent the home from having an institutional feel. The setting, design and decoration of the building can contribute to this (along with the way in which staff and management operate). The chart on the following page sets out some of the differences:

## Design features within a home

| Feature | Non-institutional | Institutional |
| --- | --- | --- |
| Corridors | • short, bright and spacious, carpeted;<br>• leading somewhere with alcoves and variety of spaces for sitting, with natural light, windows. | • long, no natural light, dimly lit;<br>• rows of similar-looking doors leading to a dead-end. |
| Individual rooms | • for single occupancy;<br>• different shapes;<br>• individually decorated and furnished in a variety of styles (chosen by residents);<br>• individualised doors and entrances. | • multi-occupancy;<br>• uniform size and shape;<br>• plain and utilitarian decoration;<br>• doors all the same with no identification. |
| Furniture within rooms | • brought in by residents themselves. | • all supplied by the home;<br>• same in every room. |
| Overall plan | • variation between parts;<br>• attractive and interesting layout. | • block arrangement;<br>• each floor and section the same. |
| Toilets and bathrooms | • en suite in residents' rooms;<br>• domestic and cosy;<br>• patterned and coloured tiles;<br>• coloured sanitary ware;<br>• domestic-style baths. | • harsh lighting;<br>• clinical appearance;<br>• cubicles in large room. |
| Communal rooms | • variety of furniture of different heights;<br>• chairs arranged with small tables;<br>• settees, carpeted. | • chairs all the same, plastic-covered;<br>• arranged around walls;<br>• drab appearance. |
| Dining facilities | • attractive setting (even if large);<br>• carpeted, with domestic-style tables and chairs. | • large, canteen-style, with plastic-topped tables and hard floor covering. |

### 8.4.4  A supportive environment

The built environment should recognise that older people may have restricted mobility or sensory impairments. Many will have dementia. Supportive features should be incorporated so as to minimise and compensate for all these difficulties. The following design characteristics are important:

- it should be easy for residents to find their way around the building. It is essential that they should be able to locate their own private space, identify how to get to a toilet wherever they are in the building, know where and how to find help and assistance, and know how to get to sitting areas;

- there should be simple, obvious routes around larger buildings, with points of interest as 'landmarks' (for example, plants or pieces of furniture) so that the individuals know where they are, and with as few dead-ends as possible;

- long featureless corridors with similar-looking doors and dead-ends are confusing and should be avoided, particularly in new build;

- there should be easy movement between all parts of the building with doors which can be opened easily and used by people in wheelchairs;

- there should be passenger lifts to upper floors big enough for wheelchairs;

- easy-to-climb stairs with handrails both sides, midway landings and seating are important;

- good levels of lighting are essential; changes of floor levels should be clearly marked, for example the edges of steps. Good lighting is important in helping to reduce confusion. Lighting which casts shadows on to floors should be avoided because they can be misinterpreted – for example, they may give the impression that there is something to step over;

- signs should be in bold, clear and large letters fixed at eye level (including for those in wheelchairs). They should contrast with door colour and include pictures as well as words. They should mean what they say; thus signs for the toilet should show a picture of a toilet rather than a man or a woman;

- when colours are used to convey information (for example, the colour of toilet doors) they should be distinctive: bright colours such as red, orange and yellow are the most effective, blue and green the least;
- doors not for use by residents should not be brightly coloured but should tone in with the surrounding wall;
- exit doors should be carefully signed and in a new building placed so as not to create confusion;
- any specially designed fixtures and fittings, for example in toilets and bathrooms, should be in as domestic-style as possible;
- the use of technology should be sensitive, for example communication systems which are non-intrusive;
- loop-hearing systems in lounges should be available;
- individual residents' doors should be personalised for easy recognition (for example, by colour, favourite object or photograph); their rooms should be personalised with their own fittings and furniture and other bits and pieces which have meaning for the individual;
- a number of smaller lounges and activity rooms rather than a single large lounge will help people to mix with each other. A view into a room, such as through an open door or room divider will make a room seem more accessible to the person approaching it;
- homes should provide a safe environment which provides a balance between over-protection and risk with unobtrusive fire and security precautions;
- there should be access to a safe and interesting garden with 'wandering' paths – that is, a route which leads a person through the garden and back into the building unobtrusively.

### 8.4.5 Pleasant environment

In addition to being functional, the building should provide a pleasant and secure environment in which to live. Attention should be paid to the aesthetic qualities of a building. For example:

- lighting, especially the maximum use of natural daylight;
- the imaginative use of colour and decorations;
- having points of interest which may provide stimulation and conversation;

- a variety of usable spaces both inside and outside the building, some of which may be semi-protected – for example, porches, conservatories.

*Gardens*

The gardens in homes are an important part of the premises. They should be safe for people to walk in, without steps (if possible) and accessible for wheelchairs. Security measures should be unobtrusive but reliable. Seats at strategic points with sheltered and shaded areas enable residents to spend time outside. Raised flowerbeds, herb gardens and greenhouses make it easier for residents to take an active interest in the garden. Fountains and ponds may be appreciated. Scented gardens are valued by people who are visually impaired. Birds and other wildlife can be encouraged.

### 8.4.6  Progressive privacy

Where a building is used for a number of purposes or as a community building (as may be the case in some larger developments), the concept of progressive privacy (physically determined stages in the building which permit increasing levels of privacy to be established) protects the privacy of residents whilst allowing the building to be used in other ways. Three types of space should be distinguished, both in terms of use, design and 'physical barriers' (for example, a door, lift, corridor or separate wing):

- *semi-public*, a partially 'open door' through which anyone in the community can pass who has a reason for doing so, for example for day care, to attend a coffee morning or to ask for information;
- *semi-private areas*, closed to outsiders and only open to people who have a reason to be in the residential area, for example residents, staff and visitors;
- *private accommodation*, open only to the individual resident. No one else should cross the threshold without seeking and gaining permission; this includes staff and visitors.

Whilst all three types of space only apply to larger establishments, the last two should apply to all homes. From a resident's standpoint, such an arrangement allows a resident 'to go out' without actually having to do so and facilitates contact between the outside world and the residents. At the same time, it recognises and protects the residents' privacy and sense of 'home'.

## 8.5    Common facilities

Facilities and space which are shared by residents should be provided in domestic-style rooms in a non-institutional and non-clinical manner. They should be interesting and varied.

### 8.5.1    Communal rooms

The amount of common space will depend on the size and nature of residents' rooms. In some cases, personal accommodation might be accorded greater priority than common space, depending on the lifestyle of residents. Two or more smaller communal rooms may be better than one large space, although this would preclude everyone gathering together on special occasions which may be important for some homes. Rooms should be well decorated and accessible for everyone. Efforts should be made to ensure that common space is welcoming. For example, too much noise is as disabling for people with dementia as steps are for someone in a wheelchair.

Within the rooms:
- chairs and furniture should be of different styles and heights;
- easy chairs should be domestic in appearance and not be covered in plastic;
- some settees should be included;
- side tables should be available (waist-height for drinks, papers, paraphernalia);
- chairs should not just be arranged around walls (unless for a special occasion or because residents prefer this) because small groupings are more homely and intimate;
- furniture should be arranged for easy access, both to allow use of wheelchairs and to provide support for those who have difficulty walking;
- fabric and furnishings should be fire-retardant.

### 8.5.2    Activity rooms

Rooms should be provided for a variety of activities. Options include:
- a quiet room and library;
- a craft room with sinks and water;
- use of functional rooms by residents, depending on their capacity and legal restrictions, for example the laundry for ironing, the kitchen(ette) for making snacks.

### 8.5.3   Connecting spaces

All corridors and entrance lobbies should:
- have level access and meet all the mobility criteria;
- have sufficient width and space for wheelchairs and walking frames (electric wheelchairs need more space);
- minimise the distance between private and communal space;
- have passenger lifts to all parts of the building with accommodation above the ground floor. These should have simple controls which can be reached from a wheelchair;
- provide a variety of spaces for sitting and looking out of a window.

One option in larger buildings may be to create an 'indoor street' instead of corridors (natural light, hard surface, external-type doors, slightly lower temperature) to give residents the impression that they are moving from their personal area to a more public one.

### 8.5.4   The needs of ethnic and other groups

In some homes, there may be special building requirements for particular groups of people. This may relate to homes wholly serving particular ethnic groups or serving a culturally mixed clientele. Such requirements might include:
- washing and toilet facilities of particular specifications;
- segregated male and female quarters;
- areas for prayer and meditation;
- requirements relating to food storage, preparation and cooking.

### 8.5.5   Toilets, bathrooms in common areas

Access to toilets in common areas should be immediately obvious either by clear signposting or by having them situated close by lounges and activity rooms. Privacy in using them is essential. Where toilets and baths/showers are not provided in individual accommodation, common facilities should be available on each floor at the following ratios:
- toilets/residents, 1:4;
- bathrooms/residents, 1:8.

Toilets should be designed to full mobility and disability standards without having a clinical appearance. Bathing equipment should be as domestic in style as possible, for example baths might have integral lifting seats. If hoists are used, care should be taken to minimise fear.

### 8.5.6 Storage space

There should be space to store luggage, spare equipment including hoists, furniture and other bulky items which are infrequently used. Proper storage should be provided for wheelchairs (including space to recharge electric wheelchairs) and walking frames. It should be out of sight and not impinge on corridors. Regulations relating to fire and safety must be observed.

## 8.6 Residents' own accommodation

The single most important aspect of living in residential care is the living accommodation provided for the individual resident. All research shows that most residents prefer a single room and that this colours their attitudes towards all other aspects of residential life. If they have to share rooms they rate lower all other elements of the service they receive.

### 8.6.1 Single occupancy

Good practice now requires that all residents in continuing care should have their own single room accommodation (unless they prefer otherwise). This applies to both residential homes and nursing homes. It is strongly recommended that single room accommodation should be a requirement for all new registrations subject to the proviso that couples, relatives or close friends are able to live together if they so wish.

### 8.6.2 Shared occupancy

Involuntary shared occupancy is never acceptable. Two people should only be living in the same accommodation if they have chosen to do so. The accommodation should be specifically designed for two people (in terms of size and facilities), paying due account to privacy. One practical option is for a couple to have two single rooms, one used as a living room, the other as a bedroom.

Arguments are sometimes advanced in favour of shared rooms, namely the benefits of companionship and the reduction of loneliness. Both these can be achieved in better ways than by relying on two strangers sharing accommodation:

- 'in a properly run and organised home loneliness should not be an issue, and certainly not a reason for anyone wanting to share;

- market forces are indicating that double rooms are proving extremely difficult to let;
- the vast majority of residents are choosing single rooms.'

From: *A Room of One's Own*, a survey of residential care homes carried out by the Association of Directors of Social Services, 1995

### 8.6.3  En suite toilet and washing facilities

It is strongly recommended that a requirement for all newly built or extended homes should be that all accommodation should have en suite toilet and washing facilities. En suite facilities should be large enough and designed to allow for help to be given in using the toilet or basin, or for a wheelchair to be used. Careful design will reduce the amount of space taken from the living area of the accommodation although it must be recognised that installing en suite facilities into existing accommodation eats into available space and can therefore only be done where practicable. There should be a washbasin and associated storage space for toiletries. Level entry showers (with a seat and a drain in the floor) may be valuable for those who enjoy them and a help for people with continence problems. Floors should have a non-slip surface and handrails should be fitted. For accommodation without en suite facilities the minimum requirement should be a washbasin in each room.

Toilets should be of a comfortable height with built-in support. Taps designed for people with weak or arthritic hands should be fitted. Advice should be sought from an occupational therapist for particular requirements.

## 8.7  Suitability of accommodation

There are a number of factors to consider when deciding whether accommodation is suitable. Most are checked prior to registration and the following provide a guide. Some should be regarded as minimum requirements while others should be included in the home's improvement programme.

### 8.7.1  Size of room

The total area of a room is one of the key input measures that is checked by inspection and registration units before registration. Whilst important, an over-concentration on size may lead to other factors being overlooked. The generally accepted minimum size is ten square metres for single accommodation. This code recommends that all homes aim to ensure that over time their provision will enable residents to have their own private rooms large enough to hold a reasonable amount of their own furniture and to accommodate all the activities of daily living that a resident can expect to carry out. This will mean that there should be room for a table and chairs, an armchair, a television and other leisure activity paraphernalia. There should be space for turning a wheelchair and for staff to provide assistance. It should also be possible to move the bed into alternative positions, including into the centre of the room should access be required from both sides for nursing care. If standard room measurements are used for planning or registration and inspection purposes, they should exclude unusable space such as low ceilings, odd corners, and en suite toilets.

In new buildings or extensions, the size of the individual's accommodation is the single greatest determinant of cost. Providers – and funders and prospective residents – will have to assess the conflicting demands of capital costs and fee levels. Compromises may need to be made. For example, if residents tend to spend much of their time in their own rooms, then it may be possible to have smaller communal areas and increase the size of individual rooms. The architecture of an already established home needs to be taken into account, especially in relation to local planning and building regulations.

*Other factors*
Other factors to consider include:
- the proportion of a room (a long narrow room may not have enough space adjacent to the bed);
- there should be adequate soundproofing to ensure residents are not unnecessarily disturbed by outside noise (for example, other people's televisions). This should not, however, be such as to make the resident feel isolated and cut off from the normal bustle of daily activity;
- where a room has a poor view such as a blank wall, efforts should be made to counteract this by, for example, planting a shrub or growing climbing plants;

- window(s) should be of an adequate size and be of good proportion in relation to size of room. Where possible the window-sill should be low enough for the resident to look out without obstructed vision when seated or when lying in bed.

### 8.7.2  Furniture

Accommodation should be large enough to contain:
- a bed (at least three feet wide) or double bed if preferred (helpful for people with dementia);
- at least one comfortable armchair (preferably two);
- a table and an upright chair which a resident can use for eating meals, writing and other leisure activities;
- storage space for clothes, for example a chest of drawers and hanging space;
- storage space for other possessions, for example shelves, cupboards;
- lockable storage for money and valuables.

### 8.7.3  Doors to individual accommodation

Doors represent, both physically and psychologically, the entrance to a resident's private space. It is important, therefore, that as far as possible the resident controls who enters, both through locks and keys and staff and visitors knocking and waiting for an invitation to enter. Doors and locks must comply with fire regulations.

*Locks*

Doors to individual accommodation should be lockable from both sides with staff holding a master key or other override mechanism in case of emergency. As far as possible, residents should hold their own keys with no restriction as to when they can lock the door. Locks on doors with residents holding keys is one of the main indicators that residents' privacy is respected.

*Opening doors*

Doors should be easy to open especially for people in wheelchairs or for people who are frail. Where appropriate, their wishes to keep doors open should be respected.

*Personalised*

The outside of doors should be sufficiently distinct and personalised so that residents can easily recognise their own door. If they wish, their doors could display their names (but in large enough type to be easily read, for example at least one centimetre high) or a wooden or pottery plaque. Other options include photographs, coloured panels, paintings, a familiar number, plant or other distinguishable feature. Doors set back in an alcove make it easier to incorporate features and reduce the institutional appearance of a corridor. A door which is easily recognised, by whatever means, is important for people with dementia.

*Letterboxes*

In some homes, letterboxes might be provided (in line with fire regulations) depending on the intellectual and physical capacity of residents. If not, other systems of delivering and receiving mail and messages personally (not to individuals whilst in a group, for example at the breakfast table) should be established.

The details described above should be considered best practice, many of which can be achieved at little extra cost within an overall improvement budget. In some cases, depending on the degree of frailty experienced by residents, particularly in nursing homes, they may be less appropriate than will generally be the case. Recognition of this, however, should not be used as a way of avoiding meeting best practice standards in most homes.

### 8.7.4 Furniture, fittings and decoration

It should be normal practice for people to bring their own suitable furniture with them when moving in on a permanent basis. They should also be able to decorate and furnish their rooms in their own style (including bedding, carpets and curtains). If not, they should be freshly decorated by the home, although this may not be reasonable where the length of the previous residence has been very short. Soft furnishings and bedding should be fireproofed or fire-retardant where possible.

Rooms which are larger than the minimum size will make it easier for people to bring in their own furniture and possessions. Familiarity with their own belongings is an important support for people with dementia. If residents do not have their own furniture or if they are staying for a short period, then homes should provide suitable domestic furniture as described above.

Rooms should be equipped to allow residents to continue a familiar lifestyle and should include (though individual requirements are likely to vary):

- sufficient electric power points, with at least two double-switched outlets set at waist-height;
- light switches set at convenient points around the room and set at waist-height so that people using wheelchairs can operate them;
- an aerial socket;
- a telephone socket, either for their own telephone line, or for linking to the home's system so that outside calls can be made and received in private;
- loop systems (for televisions, radios, music players) may be installed if cost permits.

### 8.7.5 Emergency communications system

There should be a straightforward, easy-to-use communications system for both emergency situations and minor calls, ideally voiced-based. Once activated, the system should indicate the origin of the call without disturbing other residents or staff. Communication systems should not replace personal contact by staff.

## 8.8 Environment within the home

Wherever possible, residents should be able to control the environment in their own accommodation.

### 8.8.1 Temperature

Heating systems should maintain adequate temperature and comply with all safety regulations, be controllable in sectors and, where possible, with individual control in each room. A resident should be able to choose the temperature level in his or her own accommodation. If they are resident-controlled, heating systems should be easy to understand and operate. Water temperature should comply with safety regulations.

### 8.8.2 Ventilation

Windows should be easy to open with no risk of the resident falling out. The amount of air coming in should be controllable. Size of openings should conform to building regulations in relation to rate of exchange of air within the room. There should be curtains or blinds which residents can operate easily to provide privacy at night-time and during the day when necessary.

### 8.8.3 Lighting

Different forms and type of lighting should be available, at a minimum a main room light, bedside light and direct light over chair or table. Where necessary, account should be taken of a resident's reduced vision. Trailing flexes should be avoided.

## 8.9 Technology

During the coming decade, technology will become an integral, familiar and natural part of care provision. It is important that homeowners keep up to date with new developments from which their residents and staff can benefit.

### 8.9.1 Uses

Some of its uses will be:
- as a reminder for the resident to do something: for example, that it is a meal time or to take some medication;
- as a compensation for memory loss: for example, switching off the tap if the bath is overflowing;
- as relaxation: for example, snoezelen rooms;
- as stimulation: for example, personal reminiscence videos;
- for environmental management: for example, to keep the heating at an individually comfortable level;
- for behaviour management: for example, to adjust aspects of the environment (heat or light) which are causing restlessness and agitation;
- as a reminder: for example, to shut the window when the resident goes out of the room or remind him or her to take the walking frame if it has been forgotten;
- for surveillance: for example, as a passive alarm which will increasingly be programmed individually so that it is activated only when someone does not get back into bed after fifteen minutes (but never as active surveillance, replacing staff alertness);

- for control: for example, new-style locks on doors;
- for safety: for example, passive infra-red sensors which will turn on the light when someone gets out of bed;
- for communication: for example, using video telephones to keep in touch;
- for coordination: for example, shared use of resident's records in the resident's room by all professional staff.

These new technologies will increasingly be controlled by personal computers which will make it possible to tailor the use of them to fit the individual care plan. It will also be possible to programme their use by prompting regular reviews. While the benefits will be enormous, there may be dangers which must be guarded against. The unethical use of technology is an infringement of residents' civil liberties and should be regarded in the same way as restraint and abuse.

### 8.9.2 Guidelines on the use of technology

The following guidelines should apply for the use of equipment or technology:
- it should only be used for the positive benefit of a resident which results in improvement in quality of life;
- it should be the least intrusive of equally beneficial actions: that is, simple actions should be used first;
- wherever possible it should be used only with the active consent of the resident who recognises the action as beneficial;
- any risks or side effects should be fully understood by the resident (or relatives and staff);
- proper protocols should be followed for actions which are controversial, and proper records kept (as below);
- its use and effectiveness should be reviewed at appropriate intervals;
- it should never be used solely for the convenience of staff.

The records kept should state:
- the nature of the problem being addressed;
- what methods have been used to resolve the problem;
- why a particular action or technology has been chosen;
- how long it is to be used for and a date set for its review;
- who agreed to its use and who will participate in the review.

## 8.10   The impact of design on staff

### 8.10.1  Staff rooms

Staff should have their own communal rest room where they can rest and relax between duties and also a room where training can take place when required. Care should be taken to provide a big enough space to cater for staff numbers and it should be comfortably furnished, with storage facilities for personal clothes and belongings. There should be separate toilets and washing facilities for staff. The home should have a smoking or preferably a no smoking policy which is strictly adhered to. It is well recognised that attention paid to the welfare of staff will have a beneficial effect on staff morale and on the quality of their work. Facilities provided for staff, however, should not take precedence over those provided for residents or be seen to be better than residents' facilities. Meeting standards for both should be seen as complementary activities.

### 8.10.2  Design of staff areas

Where kitchens and laundries are newly installed, account should be taken of current ergonomic standards to make for efficient and safe working. Guidance should be sought from the appropriate authorities. Minimum standards as laid down by legislation, regulations and directives must be met. Other standards should be achieved as part of the improvement programme.

# Preventing abuse

## 9.1. Introduction

The aim of this code is to promote good practice. One important element of good practice is to guard against any kind of exploitation, neglect or abuse of residents. An environment which is constantly seeking to improve the life and care of residents automatically tends to guard against bad practice.

In spite of registration, inspection, internal monitoring, quality assurance systems and codes of practice, regrettably abuse occurs. Sometimes this may be unwitting or unintentional perhaps through ignorance or neglect. At other times, however, it may be deliberate, whether subtle or overtly cruel. There is now greater recognition of the fact that abuse does occur and a fuller understanding of how it arises.

## 9.2. The definition of abuse

'Elder abuse is a single or repeated act or lack of appropriate action occurring within any relationship where there is an expectation of trust which causes harm or distress to an older person.'

*Action on Elder Abuse*

Abuse is the harming of another individual usually by someone who is in a position of power, trust or authority over that individual. The harm may be physical, psychological or emotional or it may be directed at exploiting the vulnerability of the victim in more subtle ways (for example, through denying access to people who can come to the aid of the victim, or through misuse or misappropriation of his or her financial resources). The threat or use of punishment is also a form of abuse. Abuse may happen as a 'one-off' occurrence or it may become a regular feature of a relationship. Other people may be unaware that it is happening and for this reason it may be difficult to detect. In many cases, it is a criminal offence.

### 9.2.1 Physical abuse

Rough handling or unnecessary physical force, either deliberate or unintentional, used in caring for a resident is abuse. Injuries may not always be visible although often there may be bruises, broken skin, cuts, burns or broken bones. During an episode of abuse, damage to property or clothing may also occur. Restraining residents so that they cannot move, or by shutting them in a room, is abusive. However, it may sometimes be difficult to draw the dividing line between justifiable and unjustifiable restraint.

### 9.2.2 Verbal abuse

Shouting and swearing at someone should be regarded as abusive behaviour. In addition, speaking to a resident in a quiet but threatening way so as to make the resident fearful or to make the resident an object of ridicule is equally abusive.

### 9.2.3 Emotional abuse

Playing on someone's emotions to make him or her afraid, uneasy or unnecessarily dependent is another form of abuse. Exploiting a resident through using personal information gained through the caring relationship is an abuse of the trust vested in the carer.

### 9.2.4 Abuse through the misapplication of drugs

The use of drugs to control or restrain a resident is unacceptable unless medically required. The overuse and misuse of sedatives and other medication, which too often happens in homes, should be regarded as evidence of bad practice.

### 9.2.5 Financial abuse

Financial abuse includes the improper use or control of, or the withholding of, a person's money, pension book, property, bank account or other valuables.

### 9.2.6 Racial abuse

Victimising people, verbally insulting them and physically attacking them because of their racial or ethnic origin is abusive.

### 9.2.7 Sexual abuse

Forcing someone to take part in sexual activity against his or her will is abuse and a criminal offence. The force does not have to be physical. Undue emotional pressure placed on an individual may lead him or her to acquiesce in behaviour he or she finds unacceptable.

### 9.2.8 Neglect

The withholding of care and treatment when it is required is a form of abuse. Similarly, depriving residents of the essentials of everyday life, such as food, clothes, warmth and personal cleanliness should also be regarded as a form of abuse.

## 9.3 How and why abuse might occur

There are many reasons why abuse occurs in residential and nursing homes. They range from the individual to the institutional:

- abuse may result from the actions of individual members of staff because they lack the training, experience and management support to cope with the stresses of caring for people who require a high level of assistance;
- occasionally it may occur because individual members of staff set out deliberately to harm residents;
- more often, abuse occurs because the home, its managers and staff slip, often without realising it, into a set of attitudes which reflects low morale, defensiveness about their competence and a lack of concern and respect for residents;
- overwork, lack of appreciation, low pay and low self-esteem may all contribute to the development of an environment in which abuse becomes an accepted feature of daily life.

This demonstrates clearly the need for:

- careful staff selection procedures;
- training and management support for staff once in post;
- leadership from senior management;
- the development of a working environment which values staff, does not demand too much of them and rewards them adequately.

**An environment which may provoke abuse:**

- where there are inadequate staffing levels to cope with a high incidence of incontinence;
- lack of trained and experienced care staff;
- absence of staff supervision by trained and experienced managers;
- terms and conditions of employment which do not provide holidays or guarantee other basic employment rights;
- a casual approach to resident privacy where staff walk into rooms unannounced, doors are left open when residents use the toilet, staff talk about residents over their heads or divulge confidential information.

## 9.4 Prevention

### 9.4.1 Prevention of abuse policy

All homes should have an explicit prevention of abuse policy. This will demonstrate commitment at the highest level to promoting an abuse-free environment where there are policies and practices in place which ensure that institutional abuse (that is, abuse which is fostered by poor management and staffing procedures) does not occur and that abuse by individuals is identified and eradicated (through the disciplinary process, leading to dismissal where appropriate). The policy should include:

- a statement of principle that the home is committed to preventing abuse;
- an outline of training procedures in abuse prevention;
- an outline of disciplinary procedures in the event of abuse occurring;
- information about how to use the complaints procedure if abuse occurs;
- information on the range of organisations which can provide advice and support for staff.

### 9.4.2 Staffing procedures

The quality of life in the home is underpinned by the qualities of leadership and competence shown by the homeowner and manager. Beyond that, much depends on the calibre of the staff team. It is essential that basic good practice in staff recruitment, training and supervision is observed.

This involves:

- taking up references and character checks. It is good practice to confirm written references by telephone calls;
- including specific reference to the avoidance and prevention of abuse in job descriptions to demonstrate how seriously it is taken;
- induction procedures which include going over the prevention of abuse policy;
- regular supervision sessions between manager and individual staff members to provide support in coping with stressful situations and to encourage staff;
- encouraging an atmosphere where staff feel able to discuss and therefore prevent the development of potentially abusive situations;
- assuring staff that their jobs will not be threatened if they 'blow the whistle' on abusive behaviour by other staff;
- making clear in the terms and conditions of employment and in the disciplinary procedures that abusive behaviour is a dismissable offence. Instances of serious abuse should be regarded as gross misconduct and subject to instant dismissal. Lesser forms of abuse should be subject to the normal disciplinary procedure, which if repeated would lead to dismissal;
- ensuring that professional codes of conduct are observed. In addition to the internal disciplinary procedures, sanctions imposed through such codes (for example, for nurses) will apply.

## 9.5   Action to be taken if abuse occurs

If the situation is urgent, the person witnessing the abuse should:

- immediately challenge the person who is abusing the resident, even though this may be difficult to do, and try to persuade him or her to stop;
- report the incident to a senior manager straightaway.

If the immediate risk to the resident has passed a more considered approach might be helpful. The person witnessing the abuse should:

- check which of the home's policies and guidelines have been broken, or check against this code;
- write down all the relevant facts;

- consider using the home's complaints procedure if appropriate; or
- consider the most appropriate senior member of staff to approach and whether it would be helpful to have another member of staff involved;
- ask for a confidential meeting with the most senior manager appropriate at which the abuse is raised;
- the manager should then decide what action to take (for example, invoke the disciplinary procedure, take evidence, call in the police).

If the above action does not stop the abuse, or if the home's management is involved or is unwilling to take the necessary corrective action, then the person witnessing the abuse should:

- speak to another trusted member of staff if not already involved; or
- in larger organisations, report the matter to headquarters if insufficient attention is being paid to it by managers in the home; or
- seek advice from a professional or expert organisation, a homes association or registration authority; or
- report the matter to the registration authority.

If at any time the situation involves something which is against the law, or the resident or witness is in danger, the person concerned should:

- contact the police and ask for immediate help.

## 9.6   Restraint

While restraint may sometimes be necessary, it should only be considered after all other courses of action have been exhausted. Commonly used methods of restraint include:

- cotsides;
- harnesses;
- sedatives;
- baffle locks;
- arranging furniture to impede movement;
- use of nightclothes during waking hours;
- chairs whose construction immobilises people.

If any of these methods are used inappropriately, as well as being unethical they may exacerbate dementia, enhance the risk of developing pressure sores, contribute to weight loss, osteoporosis and other harmful conditions. Guidelines produced by the Royal College of Nursing (*see Appendix 2*) suggest alternatives which include helping the person to understand his or her surroundings better and controlling the environment. When restraint is used, it should be time-limited, regularly reviewed and always be recorded in the care plan.

### 9.6.1 Neglect and litigation

The threat of litigation and accusations of neglect (by failure to restrain) may complicate the issue. Staff may feel driven to use restraint if they are frequently criticised by the resident's family. This potential threat should never be used as the rationale for determining policies or practice. These should be based on principles as outlined, for example, in this code. If these are adhered to, and should litigation be brought, the home can be confident in its ability to defend good practice and high standards. Assuming this to be the case, staff and homes should have the support of management, homes associations and registration and inspection units.

## 9.7 Other abuse

In some circumstances, staff themselves may be subject to abuse from residents or residents may abuse each other. Sexual advances and verbal abuse are not uncommon. Racist behaviour from and between residents can and does occur. Staff may find this difficult to talk about and handle. They may react inappropriately. Staff training and support systems are the key to managing such behaviour.

# Dying and death

## 10.1 Introduction

As important to residents as the quality of their lives while they are living in the home will be the way in which they are cared for during the process of dying. This means that their physical and emotional needs should be met, their comfort and well-being attended to and their wishes respected. Pain and distress should be controlled and the privacy and dignity of a resident who is dying should at all times be maintained.

## 10.2 The death of people living in residential care

The fact that most residents die in the homes they are living in rather than returning to their own homes or being moved into hospital does not mean that dying and death should be routine and commonplace. The impact of death on the community of residents will be significant and continuing and it is important to ensure that opportunities are available for them to come to terms with issues of life and death in the way that each individual finds best. This should be done by ensuring that opportunities are provided for meditation and reflection, for contact with local religious and spiritual leaders and that there is an openness and willingness on the part of staff and others involved in the home to talk about dying and death, and about those who have recently died.

### 10.2.1 Policies and procedures

The issues around dying and death are very sensitive. All homes should aim to have clearly understood operational policies which deal with quality of life before death, planning in anticipation of death and the practical and legal requirements following the death of a resident.

Consideration should be given to:

- physical, medical and nursing care (especially with regard to comfort and pain relief);
- spiritual and emotional aspects;
- cultural and religious beliefs and practices;
- legal issues and other formalities to do with death;
- relatives' and friends' involvement;
- the communal life of the home and the involvement of other residents;
- support for staff.

Policies once framed should be clearly expressed in information made available to residents and their families and friends when they first come into the home.

## 10.3 Expressed wishes of the resident

Some people will be clear about their preferences with regard to care when they are dying and the formalities to be observed after their death. They may be very ready to discuss it with those closest to them and with staff. In other cases, people may be more reluctant to broach the subject, or have it broached with them. Staff should be alert to occasions when individuals may reveal their thoughts and preferences unexpectedly so that they can make use of this when the time arises.

However it is done, the process of talking to residents about their death is a delicate one which should be done sensitively and with compassion. It may be very time-consuming.

## 10.4 Planning ahead

### 10.4.1 Information about the resident

Where possible the home, perhaps in conjunction with relatives or friends, should assemble information about the following, to be made use of at the time of the death of a resident:

- details of next of kin;
- people to be informed in case of serious illness or death;
- the existence and location of a will and next of kin instructions;

- funeral arrangements and any preferences about disposal of the body;
- the person to be responsible for making arrangements and taking responsibility for the resident's property;
- any religious or cultural practices;
- any other personal request.

Information of this sort, once gathered, should be confirmed periodically and always observed at the appropriate time.

### 10.4.2 Financial affairs, wills and next of kin instructions

Everyone should be encouraged to make a will. Help can be obtained from the local law society or citizens advice bureau. The home, managers and staff should have no involvement in residents' financial affairs or their wills other than enabling them to receive advice and help from outside sources. These matters should be handled by relatives, a solicitor, an appointee, an attorney or the Court of Protection, Court of Session or the High Court. The resident may have completed a next of kin instruction form or left other written instructions. Wherever possible, the resident's wishes should be respected and carried out.

### 10.4.3 Living wills, advance directives

A living will or an advance directive is a form of 'anticipated' consent. Someone who is rational and competent to make decisions makes a written statement about what they would like to happen if he or she becomes seriously ill and for some reason can no longer consent to or refuse treatment. This usually refers to circumstances such as brain damage or dementia. The statement usually expresses a wish that his or her life should not be artificially prolonged by medical intervention.

If residents wish to make an advance directive, they should be able to do so and to receive appropriate advice. Although not legal documents, advance directives should be honoured whenever possible. It should be noted that although an enduring power of attorney extends the power of an attorney to act when the person who made the arrangement is no longer competent to do so, the legislation specifically excludes matters of consent to or refusal of medical treatment.

## 10.5 Dying

Some people may express thoughts about dying, in particular their hope for a peaceful, pain-free death or their fear of death and their concerns for those left behind. Those who are in the position of providing care and support should do everything they can to calm these fears and attend to these concerns. Staff should adopt an approach which is honest and open about the facts of illness and death should the individual ask them.

In every home there should be particular members of staff with experience and training in looking after people who are dying who can advise other members of staff. In nursing homes, there should be nursing staff with appropriate skills in palliative care. All care staff should receive some training in looking after people who are dying and be aware of their physical and emotional needs. They should only act within their competence and know when to call upon others.

### 10.5.1 Care and comfort

It is essential that a dying person receives all the care and comfort that is required. Particular attention should be paid to keeping the person comfortable and responding to any requests. This may involve moving the person's position regularly (sitting up or lying down), keeping the person clean and cool, paying special attention to the person's mouth and giving regular drinks, and helping him or her to use the toilet. Additional staff may be required and night staff should be fully involved to make sure that care is given constantly throughout the night. An adjustable bed or ripple mattress may be helpful, and procedures such as the insertion of a catheter may be required from trained staff. Expert advice on pain control and management should be sought for all residents who need it. Medical practitioners, community nurses or specialist nurses such as Macmillan or Marie Curie nurses can provide advice and assistance. Any painkilling or respiratory drugs should be given only under the supervision of a doctor.

It is usually considered good practice that a person close to death should not be left alone, although any wish to be alone should be respected. Relatives and friends may wish to be involved, but if there are none, staff such as key workers (where they exist) have a special role to play. Other residents and ancillary staff may wish to spend time with the dying person and this should be respected if the dying person wishes it.

Above all, at all times, the privacy and dignity of the dying person should be preserved. Attending to the physical needs of the person – washing, bodily functions, feeding – should be done in private. Staff should not assume that the person cannot hear what is being said so they should never talk *about* the individual when they are in his or her presence.

## 10.6 Place of dying

Residents should be able to die in their own beds in their own rooms, surrounded by familiar people and possessions. Any additional care required should be brought into the room aiming to preserve as home-like and non-clinical environment as possible. Wherever possible, residents should not have to move away from the home to die (unless it is essential for them to go into hospital). Neither should there be a 'sick room' or 'special care unit' to which people are moved during their last days since this quickly becomes associated in residents' minds as 'the end of the road'. Following death, the person's body should not be moved from his or her own room to another part of the home before being taken away by the undertaker, nor taken away from the home in an undignified manner.

### 10.6.1 Shared rooms

Complications arise if the person who is dying is in a shared room (the position is different for couples or close friends). There can be little doubt that it is easier to provide the nursing and personal care needed by the dying resident with dignity and in privacy in a single room and without the presence of another resident. The impact of a succession of deaths for someone living in a shared room would be intolerable. Residents in a room with a dying fellow resident or where a death has occurred should if possible be offered the option of a move.

## 10.7 Hospices and hospitals

Homes should make themselves aware of the care and services which local hospices have to offer. Many have outreach services and are able to offer help in a home without the resident having to be admitted to the hospice.

Where the person is in extreme pain or has other complications, it may be better for him or her to be looked after in a hospice or a hospital. Such decisions should only be made after consultation with the person, any relatives and on medical advice. Any wishes of the resident, or advance directives, should be respected if possible. The resident should also be able to return to his or her own home if possible and if he or she so wishes.

## 10.8 Relatives' involvement

Relatives may wish to be with their dying relative and every encouragement and opportunity should be made for them to do so if this is known to be in accordance with the dying person's wishes. Space and a quiet room should be available for relatives to sit, collect their thoughts and grieve. Relatives may wish to stay in the home. This could be either in the resident's room, in separate guest accommodation or through a temporary arrangement. Meals, refreshments and other facilities should be made available. This hospitality should be extended to relatives whether they have been regular visitors or not.

Some relatives may wish to be fully involved in the care of their resident while others may just wish to be close by. Staff should ask about relatives' wishes and facilitate them.

## 10.9 Other residents

The size and nature of a home will to a certain extent dictate how the other residents are involved. In general they should be kept informed of someone's impending death and be encouraged to visit him or her if they so wish. Cultural or religious practices may be appropriate such as prayers, vigils, playing favourite music or welcoming relatives. The extent to which this happens in a corporate way will depend on custom and practice within the home and how far it accords with the dying person's wishes.

## 10.10 Staff involvement

All staff who have had any involvement with the dying resident – and this includes managerial and ancillary staff as much as it does nursing and care staff – should be kept informed when someone is dying. Those who wish should be given time to spend with the dying resident. This is one way of ensuring that there is always someone present. Support should be given to staff who have been closely involved with the resident and their emotional needs should be recognised and catered for, particularly in the case of staff who are witnessing death for the first time.

## 10.11 Death

All the necessary procedures in terms of washing, dressing and laying out the body should be undertaken sensitively and with dignity. All appropriate cultural or religious observances should be rigorously adhered to.

### 10.11.1 Inform next of kin

If the next of kin or those most closely involved were not present at the time of death, it is the responsibility of the manager to inform them as soon as possible that their relative has died.

### 10.11.2 Formal notifications and documentation

Depending on who is responsible for making the arrangements, the manager should do what is necessary or give whatever help is required to support the relatives. Whatever the position the home is likely to have a central role.

Things to do will include:
- obtaining the death certificate from the doctor;
- informing the coroner if the death was unexpected;
- registering the death;
- contacting the undertaker and making funeral arrangements.

The manager should also inform the registration authority and follow any other agreed organisational procedures.

### 10.11.3 Announcing a death

News of a resident's death should be announced in a dignified and gentle way. It may be best to announce it quietly to individuals or staff groups to begin with but some more public announcement may also be appropriate in due course. Some people may find this public recognition comforting. It should never be assumed that people with dementia do not understand when someone has died. Some of the following possibilities might be appropriate:

- a minute's silence at an appropriate time;
- a photograph or some other personal tribute in a suitable place;
- opportunity to visit the dead person and pay last respects;
- a memorial or thanksgiving service or some other religious or cultural ceremony;
- lighting a candle;
- playing a favourite piece of music or reading a poem;
- a plant, picture or piece of furniture in memory of the person. Plaques should be kept discreet so that the home is not overrun with memorials.

## 10.12 Funeral

Residents and staff should be able and helped to attend the funeral or other ceremony if they wish. Transport should be arranged and staff rotas should be adjusted either to provide escorts for residents or so that staff can attend in their own right. It may also be appropriate for the funeral cortège to leave from the home, or for it to pass the home during its journey so that residents unable to attend the funeral can pay their last respects. Depending on relatives' wishes, it may be possible for the home to offer refreshments to those who have attended the funeral so that the whole of the resident group can be involved. Alternative space and activities should be provided for residents who do not wish to be involved.

## 10.13 Bereavement

Staff should be alert to the impact the death of individual residents may have on those remaining in the home. They should be trained to recognise symptoms of grieving and learn how to respond. Formal bereavement counselling or contact with a specialist organisation may be appropriate. In the case of people with dementia, changes in their behaviour may indicate the impact the death of a fellow resident has had on them and staff should be ready to offer comfort and support.

Within a home, the loss of one of a couple, or of a close friendship needs special and sympathetic support. Particular sensitivity will be needed in some practical matters such as any change of accommodation or disposal or handing over to relatives of clothes and other belongings. These should not be rushed.

### 10.13.1 Moving into a home following bereavement

Many people come into a home after their partner has died. Staff should recognise that new residents may be going through a grieving process and they should therefore be sensitive to their sense of loss and offer support. The quality of support will be enhanced by specific training.

## 10.14 Formal and business arrangements

The agreement of residence should outline the fees payable in the case of the death of a resident. The former resident's accommodation should be available to his or her family for a reasonable period of time in order for personal possessions to be removed and affairs completed. A balance should be struck between this need and the time necessary to prepare the room for a new resident. A period of two to three weeks is likely to be needed. A final account should be rendered in accordance with the terms and conditions agreed at the outset and any valuables and property held for safekeeping should be returned to the executor.

# Ensuring standards: registration, inspection and quality assurance

## 11.1 Introduction

The procedures for ensuring standards in continuing care are both mandatory (registration and inspection) and voluntary (quality assurance). The way in which these procedures have a bearing on this code are described in the following sections.

## 11.2 Registration

Local authorities and health authorities are responsible for registering residential care homes and nursing homes respectively. The registration authorities must ensure that the purposes and aims of establishments are clearly set out and that the standards of care they offer match these aims and objectives. They have a duty to ensure that the best quality of life for residents is achieved.

### 11.2.1 Registration process

Registration authorities should set out the registration requirements in general terms. This is best done in the form of a guide, listing key documents relating to the registration process. Throughout this process, registration staff will need to be available to monitor progress and preparations for the opening of the home. Advice may need to be given to proprietors about the initial selection of residents, selection of staff, preparation of a home brochure, and to ensure that the registration requirements agreed initially are being implemented.

Prospective owners/managers should be reminded that there are penalties for operating an unregistered home and residents must not be admitted until a certificate of registration is issued. Certificates of registration should be issued as soon as possible but the process of checking fitness has to be done thoroughly and may take time.

### 11.2.2 The suitability of applicants for registration

Registration authorities must ensure that all prospective owners/managers of homes possess some relevant qualifications or have some proven experience of employment within residential care. They should also be able to demonstrate competence in and understanding of financial projections and budgeting. They should show that they possess a business-like approach which will ensure that any new home will be managed on a secure financial basis which will not put the future welfare of residents at risk. Where the registration authority receives applications for registration from voluntary organisations, the local, regional or national chairman, secretary or like person of the management committee of the home is registered, together with the home's manager or administrator. The registration authority should ascertain the actual and legal divisions of responsibility within the organisation. Notification of any changes of those personnel should be made to the authority once the home is registered. The registration authority should ensure that a check is made on the Department of Health national list of people who have been deregistered.

### 11.2.3 Dual registration

When an owner wishes or is required to apply for dual registration as a residential care home and nursing home, the applicant must be able to satisfy the registration authority that the requirements of the regulations will be met within the home, and should satisfy both authorities that the recommendations of this code will be followed.

### 11.2.4 Change of owner or manager of a home

Once the initial certificate of registration has been issued, owners should notify the registration authority of any intended change of ownership. Registrations are not automatically transferred to new owners or managers. New applications must be lodged and references taken up. Residents and, where they wish it, their relatives should be fully informed of any changes. This is particularly crucial where there has been a close relationship formed between the owner/manager and the residents in his or her care.

### 11.2.5 Change of facilities or objectives

Conditions of registration relating to the age, gender, number and category of residents must be adhered to. If the registered person fails to abide by these conditions he or she may be prosecuted or have his or her registration cancelled. The registration authority must be informed of any proposed changes so that the validity of registration can be considered in the new circumstances. Once changes have been approved, the home's brochure should be altered so that it describes the new situation accurately.

### 11.2.6 Cancellation of registration

In circumstances where a registration authority is considering cancelling the registration of a home, the registration authority is required to serve notice of intention to cancel registration on the registered person and must spell out the grounds for doing so. The registered person has fourteen days to indicate a wish to make representation in writing or orally to an appeals sub-committee of the local authority (residential care homes) or to a committee of the health authority (nursing homes).

If cancellation is confirmed, the registered person has a right of appeal. The Registered Homes Act 1984 provides for appeals against decisions of registration authorities to be made to registered homes tribunals. Such appeals must be made within twenty-eight days of the decision to cancel registration being notified. Registration authorities should make owners aware of their right to appeal and the procedure to be followed.

The cancellation of registration cannot take effect until either twenty-eight days have elapsed with no appeal, or the tribunal has reached its decision. The decision of the tribunal is final.

At an appropriate stage, residents, next of kin, or key supporters should be notified that cancellation of registration may come into effect. It is also essential to notify any sponsoring agencies that it may be necessary for them to make alternative accommodation arrangements for residents.

## 11.3 Inspection

Under the Residential Care Homes (Amendment) Regulations 1988 and the Nursing Homes Regulations 1984, homes must be inspected by the local authority (residential homes) and district health authority (nursing homes). Since 1991 all local authorities have been required to have in place 'arms length' inspection units with the statutory duty to register and inspect services within the independent sector and to inspect local authority residential care homes. Under the Registered Homes (Amendment) Act 1991, registration authorities must also register small care homes providing personal care to fewer than four people. Nursing homes have always been required to register if they provide care to one or more persons.

All registered homes and (since 1991) local authority homes must be inspected twice a year although registration authorities may choose to visit more often. At least one visit should be unannounced. This is essential following an anonymous or specific complaint made to an authority about poor standards of care in a home. Where an owner or company owns several homes, the registration authority may need to make such a visit to satisfy itself that the homes' managers are receiving adequate supervision and support. Inspections should be carried out by persons authorised to do so by the relevant registration authority. Inspections will vary in content, focus and length of time depending on any outstanding issues identified on previous inspections. Following initial registration, a visit of inspection should be made within the first three months of the home becoming established, or when a new manager of a home has been appointed. In the case of dual registration, it is advisable for joint inspections to take place. For this reason, the growth in the numbers of joint inspection units in recent years is to be welcomed.

Inspectors should focus on quality of care and quality of life issues as much as on the fabric of the building. Time should be devoted to asking residents and staff about standards of care provided. Care should be taken to ensure that courtesy, diplomacy and tact are used in inspecting individual residents' private rooms. The owner or manager of the home must make it possible for the inspection officer to spend some time in private with individual residents. Normally it should be possible for inspections to be conducted in a way which is seen to be constructive by managers and staff of the home. Recognition should be given to innovative and good care practice. Time should be given to discussing and reviewing, with the owner or manager, the objectives of the home and how the care of the residents can be enhanced.

At the inspection any change of circumstances affecting the registration will need to be identified. The authority should ensure that a report of the inspection is sent to the owner and the manager, drawing attention to any specific points of consultation and specifying any variation in the registration requirements. The inspection reports of residential care homes must be available to the public.

Inspectors appointed by registration authorities to undertake inspection of residential and nursing homes, to give advice to staff and be responsible to the respective registration authorities for recommendations concerning registration should be knowledgeable and skilled in communicating with owners and managers from a wide range of backgrounds. They should have sufficient experience and status to merit the respect of both colleagues and staff of homes. Many authorities now require inspectors to have had some direct experience of running or managing residential and nursing homes themselves.

## 11.4 Complaints procedures

Residential care homes are required under the 1984 regulations to have a complaints procedure in place. While there is no statutory requirement for nursing homes to do this, it is good practice to do so. The complaints procedure should be outlined in the home's brochure.

The majority of complaints regarding the management of a home will normally be satisfactorily resolved by the owner or manager and there will be no need for the registration authority to be involved.

When complaints cannot be resolved internally the registration authority should be informed of the complaint. All complaints regarding a specific home should initially be made in writing to the registration authority, giving details of any action already taken and with whom the matter has been discussed. The registration authority will then take the necessary steps to investigate the complaint and arrange to interview the owner/manager, resident and all other people relevant to the specific complaint. Following the investigation/interview, a letter should be sent to the owner and manager, resident and the complainant stating the outcome and specifying any action.

## 11.5   Consumer advice

The registration authority must make available for consultation a list of all private and voluntary homes currently registered in its area. Many authorities have also found it helpful to publish a more detailed list of registered homes describing their individual characteristics and specific services provided, such as levels of staffing and medical cover provided within the home. General information can also be given on how to obtain advice about financial assistance towards the cost of accommodation, and on the difference between a private and voluntary home and between a residential care home and a nursing home. Enquirers and prospective residents should also be reminded to request a copy of the home's brochure when seeking initial information from an owner or manager.

## 11.6   Quality assurance (QA)

Quality assurance is the process whereby service providers and those receiving care can assess the services to check that acceptable standards are being met. This can be done through self-assessment or by bringing in an outside body to conduct the assessment. In order for this process to work, agreed standards have to be set before any assessment can take place. Performance against those standards can then be measured through the quality assurance process. This code can provide the basis for setting the standards.

### 11.6.1  The benefits of QA

There are many benefits for homes which establish quality assurance procedures. QA requires managers and staff to agree what constitutes acceptable standards of care and assists them in setting up processes for monitoring their progress towards achieving them. Drawing up and agreeing standards should involve all those concerned, including residents. The day-to-day experience of those who live and work in the home should provide the starting point for the process. Essential to the process of quality assurance is the idea of self-audit or self-assessment whereby managers and staff systematically examine the service they provide, assess their performance against standards which they have already agreed in conjunction with residents, and then make adjustments and improvements where performance is shown to be deficient. Establishing a group, involving staff and residents within the home, to be responsible for quality assurance is an important first step. The QA process can be undertaken even where an outside assessor is not called in to do a formal assessment. Quality assurance should involve all members of staff at every level. Through this, standards are raised and teamworking is developed.

### 11.6.2 QA systems

There are a range of QA systems which can be used in continuing care settings. The following are examples:

- Inside Quality Assurance, developed by the Centre for Environmental and Social Studies on Ageing (CESSA);
- BS5750/ISO9000;
- QA systems established by a number of registered homes associations (for example, British Federation of Care Home Proprietors (BFCHP), National Care Homes Association (NCHA), Association of Approved Registered Care Homes (AARCH), Registered Nursing Home Association (RNIIA);
- Investors in People;
- King's Fund Organisational Audit;
- Homes are for living in (HAFLI), Social Services Inspectorate;
- Health Services Accreditation.

*(See Appendix 3 for addresses of relevant organisations.)*

### 11.6.3 Accreditation

In a climate where deregulation has increasingly been favoured, other options for ensuring standards, besides statutory inspection, may need to be considered. Accreditation is a formal system (which may be mandatory or voluntary) which provides an external and objective assessment of service quality. The accrediting body requires service providers to meet standards which are laid down and in return confers accredited status to those who achieve them. Accreditation of homes may become the acceptable way of assuring quality of care. In the future, homes could be expected to apply for accreditation by being able to demonstrate that they have reached the required standard and then submit themselves for renewal of that accredited status periodically. Accreditation is generally seen as an accepted way of ensuring that standards are met in a deregulated, market-driven environment. Purchasers would only enter into contracts with providers who were accredited and private individuals would have clear guidance on which care providers were up to standard. Existing quality assurance systems may become the basis for future accreditation systems although, in some cases, homes associations are already introducing their own systems.

# Appendix 1 – relevant legislation

The legislation which governs the establishment and running of homes and the general provision of community care services is listed below.

## General

### The Registered Homes Act 1984

This covers residential care homes in Part I and nursing homes in Part II. Under an amendment in 1991, small residential care homes of fewer than four people were also required to be registered. Separate regulations were issued to accompany each part of the Act:

- *Residential Care Homes Regulations 1984;*
  *amended in 1988* to require at least two inspections per year (of which one should be unannounced in accordance with LAC(88)15), and to require a record to be kept of valuables and money being looked after by the home on behalf of the residents;
  *amended in 1991* to require new applicants to provide birth certificates to verify their identities when police are checking them;
- *Nursing Homes and Mental Nursing Homes Regulations 1984;*
  *amended in 1988* to change the level of fees payable to the registration authority.

The Department of Health issued two circulars in 1995 relating to the regulation of residential care and nursing homes which set out current approaches to regulation and deregulation with a view to minimising paperwork and ensuring consistency of enforcement practice across sectors:

- LAC(95)12 – residential care homes;
- HSG(95)41 – nursing homes.

### NHS and Community Care Act 1990

*Sections 42-45* enable local authorities to employ voluntary organisations and private concerns as agents in providing welfare services such as residential care; preserve the rights of people already in voluntary and private homes when the new community care arrangements came into effect; govern the charging for accommodation;

*Section 46* requires local authorities to draw up plans for community care services;

*Section 47* requires local authorities to assess the care needs of any person appearing to need community care services;

*Section 48* requires inspection of premises used for provision of community care services other than registered residential care and nursing homes.

## Mental Health Act 1983
*Section 115* empowers approved social workers to enter and inspect any premises where a mentally disordered person is living if there is reason to believe he or she is not under proper care.

## Chronically Sick and Disabled Persons Act 1970

## Disabled Persons (Services, Consultation and Representation) Act 1986

## Carers (Recognition and Services) Act 1995
enables local authorities to assess the needs of carers as well as individuals thought to be in need of community care services.

## Race Relations Act 1976
*Sections 20 and 22(2)(b)* makes unlawful for anyone providing accommodation to the public, or a section of the public, in a hotel, boarding house or other similar establishment, or the services of any trade or business, to discriminate directly or indirectly against a person on racial grounds (colour, race, nationality or ethnic or national origins). There are some exemptions.

## Rehabilitation of Offenders Act 1974 ( Exemptions) Order 1975

## Employment Protection (Consolidation) Act 1978

## Registered Homes Tribunal Rules 1984
governs procedures of Tribunals which hear appeals against decisions to refuse or cancel registration.

## Scotland

**The Social Work (Scotland) Act 1968**
amended by
**The Registered Establishments (Scotland) Act 1987**

**Nursing Homes Registration (Scotland) Act 1938**
amended by
**Nursing Homes (Scotland) Amendment Act 1992**

**Mental Health (Scotland) Act 1984**

**Town and County Planning (Scotland) Act 1972**

**The Building (Scotland) Acts, 1959 and 1970**
*The Building Standards (Scotland) Regulations 1981*
*(and amendment regulations 1982 and 1984)*

## Northern Ireland

**Chronically Sick and Disabled Persons (Northern Ireland) Act 1978**

*Mental Health ( Northern Ireland) Order 1986*

*Health and Personal Social Services (Northern Ireland) Order 1972*
*(Schedule b)*

## Fire safety

Fire safety is exercised through the statutory provisions relating to registration. In reality, this usually results in the registration authorities wanting to be satisfied that fire recommendations have been met before a certificate of registration will be issued. The Residential Care Homes Regulations 1984 state the following in respect of fire safety: 'the person registered shall, at such times as may be agreed with the fire authority, consult that authority on fire precautions in the home.' The Nursing Homes and Mental Nursing Homes Regulations 1984 require comments from the fire authority to be submitted with the application for registration.

*Relevant legislation, guidance and information:*

**Fire Precautions Act 1971**

*Residential Care Homes Regulations 1984*

*Nursing Homes and Mental Nursing Homes Regulations 1984*

*Home Office/Scottish Office*
Draft guide to fire precautions in existing residential care premises and Draft guide to fire precautions in hospitals.
(January 1983-LAC(83)4; Welsh Office circular 9/84)

*Building Regulations 1991*
*BS 5588: Part 8: 1988* Code of Practice for means of escape for disabled people.
*BS 5839: Part 1: 1988 (1991)* Fire detection and alarm systems in buildings: code of practice for system design, installation and servicing.

**Furniture and Furnishings (Fire Safety) Regulations 1988**

## General safety and health and safety at work

Procedures relating to planning approval, building regulations, approved fire precautions and requirements of the environmental health services, electrical/gas and lift safety requirements must all be observed. In addition, under the Health and Safety at Work Act 1974 officers of the Health and Safety Executive are responsible for inspecting homes in relation to the health and safety of staff. The requirements include the maintenance of safe working procedures and conditions, as well as the need to record accidents and to notify the Executive of any serious incidents which have occurred. In addition, all accidents involving residents should be recorded in writing with a summary of the circumstances and a signed statement from a witness. A series of health and safety regulations came into effect in 1993 governing and updating workplace health and safety, including manual handling regulations and the provision and use of workplace equipment.

*Relevant legislation, guidance and information:*

**Health and Safety at Work Act 1974**

**Environmental Protection Act 1990**
Under the Act, there is a general duty of care with regard to the handling and disposal of waste.

*Reporting of Injuries, Diseases and Dangerous Occurrences Regulations 1985*

*Health and Safety (First-Aid) Regulations 1981*

*Control of Substances Hazardous to Health COSHH Regulations 1988*

*Manual Handling Regulations 1992*

*Management of Health and Safety at Work Regulations 1992*

*Provision and Use of Work Equipment Regulations 1992*

*Royal College of Nursing*
Code of practice for the handling of patients.

*Health and Safety Executive*
Health and safety in residential care homes.

*Health Building Note – Accommodation for Elderly People*

## Food hygiene

The Residential Care Homes Regulations 1984 include the requirement to provide adequate facilities for the storage, cooking and service of food and to supply adequate food for every resident. All residential homes also have to conform to the requirements of the Food Hygiene (General) Regulations 1970 and subsequent legislation.

*Relevant legislation, guidance and information:*

**Food Act 1984**

**Food Safety Act 1990**

*Food Hygiene (General) Regulations 1970*

*Building Regulations 1985*

## Drugs

Both the 1984 Nursing Homes and Mental Nursing Homes Regulations and the 1984 Residential Care Homes Regulations require the person registered to make adequate arrangements for the recording, safe keeping, handling and disposal of drugs.

*Relevant legislation, guidance and information:*

**Medicines Act 1968**

**Misuse of Drugs Act 1971**

*Residential Care Homes Regulations 1984*

*Nursing Homes and Mental Nursing Homes Regulations 1984*

*Misuse of Drugs Regulations 1973*

*Misuse of Drugs (Safe Custody) Regulations 1973*

*National Association of Health Authorities and Trusts (NAHAT)* Model Guidelines 1993

# Appendix 2 – further reading

Association of Directors of Social Services (1995) *Mistreatment of older people: a discussion document*. ADSS, Northallerton.

Clough, J. (1995) *Caring with competence: a practical introduction to care – an in-service development programme for staff working in residential care homes for older people*. Winslow, Bicester.

Counsel and Care
> (1992) *What if they hurt themselves*. Counsel and Care, London.
> (1993) *Sound barriers*. Counsel and Care, London.
> (1995) *Last rights*. Counsel and Care, London.

Croner's (regularly updated) *Care home management*. Croner's Publications Ltd, Kingston upon Thames.

Department of Health, Social Services Inspectorate (1989) *Homes are for living in (HAFLI)*. HMSO, London.

Health and Safety Executive (1993) *Health and safety in residential care homes*, Health and Safety Series booklet HS(G) 104. HSE Books, Sheffield.

Kellaher, L. and Peace, S. (1993) Rest assured: new moves in quality assurance for residential care *in* Johnson, J. and Slater, R., eds, *Ageing and later life*. OU Press and Sage, London.

McKay, C. and Patrick, H. (1995) *The care maze: the law and your rights to community care in Scotland*. ENABLE/Scottish Association for Mental Health, Glasgow.

National Association of Health Authorities [and Trusts] (1985) *Registration and inspection of nursing homes: a handbook for health authorities*. NAHA, Birmingham, plus Supplement, 1993.

Nazarko, L. (1996) *NVQs in nursing and residential homes*. Blackwell Science, Oxford.

Norman, A. (1987) *Rights and risk: a discussion document on civil liberty in old age*, Centre for Policy on Ageing, London.

O'Kell, S. (1995) *Care standards in the residential care sector – quality and qualifications: implications for users, providers and purchasers.* YPS/Joseph Rowntree Foundation, York.

Royal College of Nursing (1992) *Focus on restraint: guidelines on the use of restraint in the care of older people.* RCN, London.

Wagner Development Group (1990) *Staffing in residential homes: a handbook of guidance on the calculation of staffing establishments and the deployment of staff for managers, proprietors, employers and trades union officers.* NISW, London.

Worsley, J. (1992) *Good care management: a guide to setting up and managing a residential home.* ACE Books, Age Concern, London.

# Appendix 3 – useful addresses

Action on Elder Abuse
Astral House
1268 London Road
London SW16 4ER
Tel: 0181-679 2648

Advisory, Conciliation and
Arbitration Service
27 Wilton Street
London SW1X 7AZ
Tel: 0171-210 3000

Age Concern England
Astral House
1268 London Road
London SW16 4ER
Tel: 0181-679 8000

Alzheimer's Disease Society
Gordon House
10 Greencoat Place
London SW1P 1PH
Tel: 0171-306 0606

Association of British Insurers
51 Gresham Street
London EC2V 7HQ
Tel: 0171-600 3333

Association for Continence
Advice
Winchester House
Kennington Park
Cranmer Road
The Oval
London SW9 6EJ
Tel: 0171-820 8113

British Association for Service to
the Elderly (BASE)
The Guildford Institute of the
University of Surrey
Ward Street
Guildford GU1 4LH
Tel: (01483) 451036

British Council of Organisations
of Disabled People
Litchurch Plaza
Litchurch Lane
Derby DE24 8AA
Tel: (01332) 295551

British Deaf Association
38 Victoria Place
Carlisle CA1 1HU
Tel: (01228) 48844

British Diabetic Association
10 Queen Anne Street
London W1M 0BD
Tel: 0171-323 1531

British Geriatrics Society
1 St Andrews Place
Regents Park
London NW1 4LB
Tel: 0171-935 4004

Carers National Association
20-25 Glasshouse Yard
London EC1A 4JS
Tel: 0171-490 8818

Centre for Accessible
Environments
Nutmeg House
Gainsford Street
London SE1 2NY
Tel: 0171-357 8182

Centre for Environmental and
Social Studies on Ageing
University of North London
Ladbroke House
62-66 Highbury Grove
London N5 2AD
Tel: 0171-753 5038

Centre for Policy on Ageing
25-31 Ironmonger Row
London EC1V 3QP
Tel: 0171-253 1787

Chartered Society of
Physiotherapy
14 Bedford Row
London WC1R 4ED
Tel: 0171-242 1941

College of Occupational
Therapists
6-8 Marshalsea Road
London SE1 1HL
Tel: 0171-357 6480

Commission for Racial Equality
Elliott House
10-12 Allington Street
London SW1E 5EH
Tel: 0171-828 7022

Continuing Care Conference
12 Little College Street
London SW1P 3SH
Tel: 0171-222 1265

Counsel and Care
Twyman House
16 Bonny Street
London NW1 9PG
Tel: 0171-485 1566

Court of Protection
The Public Trust Office
Stewart House
24 Kingsway
London WC2 6JX
Tel: 0171-269 7000

Disabled Living Centres Council
Winchester House
Kennington Park
Cranmer Road
The Oval
London SW9 6EJ
Tel: 0171-820 0567

Disabled Living Foundation
380-384 Harrow Road
London W9 2HU
Tel: 0171-289 6111

Elderly Accommodation
Counsel
46a Chiswick High Road
London W4 1SZ
Tel: 0181-995 8320

Equal Opportunities
Commission
Overseas House
Quay Street
Manchester M3 3HN
Tel: 0161-833 9244

Federation of Small Businesses
(National Federation of Self
Employed and Small
Businesses Ltd)
140 Lower Marsh
Westminster Bridge
London SE1 7AE
Tel: 0171-928 9272

Health and Safety Executive
The Information Centre
Broad Lane
Sheffield S3 7HQ
Tel: 0114-289 2345

Health Services Accreditation
Rutherford Park
Marley Lane
Battle TN33 0EZ
Tel: (01424) 772277

Hearing Concern
7-11 Armstrong Road
London W3 7JL
Tel: 0181-743 1110

Help the Aged
St James's Walk
Clerkenwell Green
London EC1R 0BE
Tel: 0171-253 0253

Investors in People UK
4th Floor
7-10 Chandos Street
London W1M 9DE
Tel: 0171-467 1900

King's Fund Organisational
Audit
11-13 Cavendish Square
London W1M 0AN
Tel: 0171-307 2400

National Association of Health
Authorities and Trusts
Birmingham Research Park
Vincent Drive
Birmingham B15 2SQ
Tel: 0121-471 4444

Mobility Advice and Vehicle
Information Service (MAVIS)
Transport Research Laboratory
Crowthorne
Berks RG45 6AU
Tel: (01344) 770456

National Association of
Citizens Advice Bureaux
Myddelton House
115-123 Pentonville Road
London N1 9LZ
Tel: 0171-833 2181

National Association of
Inspection and Registration
Officers
28 Broom Lane
Rotherham S60 3EL
Tel: (01709) 366237

National Council for Hospice
and Specialist Palliative Care
Services
59 Bryanston Street
London W1A 2AZ
Tel: 0171-611 1153

National Council for Voluntary
Organisations
Regents Wharf
8 All Saints Street
London N1 9RL
Tel: 0171-713 6161

National Inspection Unit
Managers Group
The Inspection Unit
Friary House
Friary Park
Friern Barnet Lane
London N20 0NR
Tel: 0181-361 2525

National Listening Library,
incorporating Talking Books
12 Lant Street
London SE1 1QH
Tel: 0171-407 9417

Parkinson's Disease Society
22 Upper Woburn Place
London WC1H 0RA
Tel: 0171-383 3513

Qualifications for Work Division
(National Vocational
Qualifications)
Department of Education and
Employment
The Moor
Moorfoot
Sheffield S1 4PQ
Tel: 0114-275 3275

The Relatives Association
5 Tavistock Place
London WC1H 9SN
Tel: 0171-916 6055

Royal Association of Disability
and Rehabilitation (RADAR)
12 City Forum
250 City Road
London EC1V 8AF
Tel: 0171-250 3222

Royal College of Nursing
20 Cavendish Square
London W1M 0AB
Tel: 0171-409 3333

Royal Institute of Public Health
and Hygiene
28 Portland Place
London W1N 4DE
Tel: 0171-580 2731

Royal National Institute for the
Blind
224 Great Portland Street
London W1N 6AA
Tel: 0171-388 1266

Royal National Institute for Deaf People
19-23 Featherstone Street
London EC1Y 8SL
Tel: 0171-296 8000

Social Services Inspectorate
Department of Health
Richmond House
79 Whitehall
London SW1A 2NS
Tel: 0171-210 5569

Society of Nurse Inspection and Registration Officers
Royal College of Nursing
20 Cavendish Square
London W1M 0AB
Tel: 0171-409 3333

*Care Homes Associations and Organisations*

The Abbeyfield Society
53 Victoria Street
St Albans AL1 3UW
Tel: (01727) 857536

Anchor Trust
Fountain Court
Oxford Spires Business Park
Kidlington OX5 1NZ
Tel: (01865) 854000

Association of Approved Registered Care Homes
Central Office
Thomas Watson House
Northumberland Street
Darlington DL3 7HJ
Tel: (01325) 467847

Association of Residential Care
ARC House
Marsden Street
Chesterfield S40 1JY
Tel: (01246) 555043

British Health Care Association
24a Main Street
Garforth
Leeds LS25 1AA
Tel: 0113-232 0903

British Federation of Care Home Proprietors
840 Melton Road
Thurmaston
Leicester LE4 8BN
Tel: 0116-264 0095

The Care Forum
Ringwood House
Walton Street
Aylesbury HP21 7QP
Tel: (01296) 393055

Hanover Housing Association
Hanover House
18 The Avenue
Egham TW20 9AB
Tel: (01784) 438361

Independent Healthcare Association
22 Little Russell Street
London WC1A 2HT
Tel: 0171-430 0537

Institute of Community Care
Management
PO Box 58
Corby NN17 1ZX
Tel: (01536) 204222 ext 230

The Leonard Cheshire
Foundation
26-29 Maunsel Street
London SW1P 2QN
Tel: 0171-828 1822

Methodist Homes for the Aged
Epworth House
Stuart Street
Derby DE1 2EQ
Tel: (01332) 296200

National Care Homes
Association
3rd Floor, Martin House
84-86 Grays Inn Road
London WC1X 8BQ
Tel: 0171-831 7090

Registered Nursing Home
Association
Calthorpe House
Hagley Road
Edgbaston
Birmingham B16 8QY
Tel: 0121-454 2511

United Care Association
132 Bournemouth Road
Chandlers Ford
Eastleigh SO53 3AL
Tel: (01703) 255794

## Scotland

Age Concern Scotland
113 Rose Street
Edinburgh
EH2 3DT
Tel: 0131-220 3345

Alzheimer Scotland – Action on
Dementia
8 Hill Street
Edinburgh
EH2 3JZ
Tel: 0131-225 1453

Carers National Association
(Scotland)
11 Queen's Crescent
Glasgow G4 9AS
Tel: 0141-333 9495

Citizens Advice Scotland
26 George Square
Edinburgh EH8 9LD
Tel: 0131-667 0156

Dementia Service Development
Centre
University of Stirling
Stirling FK9 4LA
Tel: 01786 467740

Disability Scotland
Princes House
5 Shandwick Place
Edinburgh EH2 4RG
Tel: 0131-229 8632

Help the Aged Scotland
Herriot House
Herriothill Terrace
Edinburgh EH7 4DY
Tel: 0131-556 4666

Royal National Institute for the
Blind (Scotland)
10 Magdala Crescent
Edinburgh EH12 5BE
Tel: 0131-313 1498

Royal National Institute for Deaf
People
9 Clairmont Gardens
Glasgow G3 7LW
Tel: 0141-332 0343

Scottish Council for Voluntary
Organisations
18-19 Claremont Crescent
Edinburgh EH7 4QD
Tel: 0131-556 3882

Scottish Law Commission
140 Causewayside
Edinburgh EH9 1PR
Tel: 0131-668 2131

Social Work Services
Inspectorate
James Craig Walk
Edinburgh EH3 1BA
Tel: 0131-556 8400

## Northern Ireland

Age Concern Northern Ireland
3 Lower Crescent
Belfast BT7 1NR
Tel: (01232) 245729

Carers National Association for
Northern Ireland
Regional Office
113 University Street
Belfast BT7 1HP
Tel: (01232) 439843

Department of Health and Social
Services (Northern Ireland)
Dundonald House
Upper Newtownards Road
Belfast BT4 3SF
Tel: (01232) 520000

Equal Opportunities
Commission for Northern
Ireland
Chamber of Commerce House
22 Great Victoria Street
Belfast BT2 7BA
Tel: (01232) 242752

Help the Aged Northern Ireland
Lesley House
Shaftesbury Square
Belfast BT2 7DB
Tel: (01232) 230666

Office of Care and Protection
(Northern Ireland)
Royal Court of Justice
PO Box 410
Chichester Street
Belfast BT1 3JF
Tel: (01232) 235111

**Wales**

Age Concern Cymru
4th Floor
1 Cathedral Road
Cardiff CF1 9SD
Tel: (01222) 371566

Alzheimer's Disease Society
Wales Development Office
Tonna Hospital
Tonna
Neath SA11 3LX
Tel: (01639) 641938

Carers National Association in
Wales
Pantglas Industrial Estate
Bedwas
Newport NP1 8DR
Tel: (01222) 880176

Disability Wales
Llys Ifor
Crescent Road
Caerphilly CF83 1XL
Tel: (01222) 887325

Welsh Consumer Council
Castle Buildings
Womanby Street
Cardiff CF1 2BN
Tel: (01222) 396056

# Index